# AROUND THE TABLE

EXPLORING VOCATION, SERVICE
COMMUNITY AND LEADERSHIP

## JOHN W. KYLE

TFI Press
8227 Old Courthouse Road, Suite 320
Vienna, Virginia 22182
United States of America

© 2024 by The Fellows Initiative. All rights reserved. No part of this book may be reproduced in any form without written permission from the publisher.

TFI Press™ is the publishing division of The Fellows Initiative™, a network of Christian discipleship and leadership development programs for recent college graduates. TFI's mission is to inspire and equip the emerging generation of leaders for the marketplace, church, and society. TFI Fellows programs share a commitment to Jesus Christ, his Word, and his church. We encourage Fellows to live lives of servant leadership marked by the seamless integration of faith, work, service, and community. We are committed to promoting biblical flourishing in the world. All net proceeds from the sale of this book go to TFI for the advancement of its mission. For more information, visit the TFI website at www.thefellowsinitiative.org.

Unless otherwise indicated, all Scripture quotations are from the ESV® Bible (The Holy Bible, English Standard Version®), copyright © 2001 by Crossway, a publishing ministry of Good News Publishers. Used by permission. All rights reserved.

Scripture quotations marked (NIV) are taken from the Holy Bible, New International Version®, NIV®. Copyright © 1973, 1978, 1984, 2011 by Biblica, Inc.™ Used by permission of Zondervan. All rights reserved worldwide. www.zondervan.com. "NIV" and "New International Version" are trademarks registered in the United States Patent and Trademark Office by Biblica, Inc.™

ISBN 979-8-9897231-0-2 (Paperback)

# CONTENTS

| | |
|---|---|
| Introduction | 1 |
| **VOCATION** | 7 |
|     Called to Follow | 9 |
|     Called to Love | 19 |
|     Called to Think | 29 |
|     Called to Receive God's Word | 41 |
|     Called to Work and Contribute to Flourishing | 51 |
|     Called to Rest | 65 |
| **SERVICE** | 77 |
|     Called to Serve | 79 |
|     Justice and Mercy: First Principles of Service | 91 |
|     Called to Generosity | 105 |
|     Finding Joy in Service | 117 |
|     Work as Service | 127 |
|     He Came to Serve | 139 |
| **COMMUNITY** | 149 |
|     Called to Community | 151 |
|     Vulnerability and Shame | 163 |
|     One Another Passages | 173 |
|     Called to Life in the Church | 183 |
|     Peacemaking | 195 |
|     Unity and Like-Mindedness | 207 |
| **LEADERSHIP** | 219 |
|     Called to Lead | 221 |
|     Ambassadorship | 231 |
|     Sacrificial Leadership | 243 |

| | |
|---|---|
| Inspiring Others | 253 |
| Leading in the Church | 263 |
| Final Reflections | 273 |
| Acknowledgements | 277 |

# INTRODUCTION

## A VISION FOR ROUNDTABLE

Welcome to the grand adventure of your Fellows program! Something shared by all TFI programs is the weekly gathering of fellows, usually called Roundtable. Some call it Family Life Together or Commons. Regardless of the name, the goal is the same: a weekly gathering to share a meal, fellowship, and intentional conversation. It is designed to be habit-forming and something that will carry over to the next season of your life beyond the Fellows program. It is meant to be a time of vulnerability, sharing thoughts and experiences of real life so that you might minister to one another and grow together. We are on a great adventure to explore who God is and who we are, what He is doing, and what he is calling us to do. The weekly Roundtable is part of an invitation to share life with one another — real life with all its challenges and joys.

Have you considered that others in your Fellows class are a gift from God to you? God abounds with gifts. He loves us so much that he gave us his son (John 3:16). He showed his love again by giving us his Spirit (John 14:16-17). In addition, he also gives us to each other. In his sovereign wisdom, he has chosen the members of your Fellows class this year. What does it mean that you were brought together for this purpose? To explore this question, we will be looking at the "one another" passages of the Bible later in this book. For now, we can briefly consider four of them. First, we are brought together to encourage one another (I Thessalonians 5:11). Part of being in fellowship as God's people is that we are all part of the ministry of encouragement, to build one another up in the faith despite the challenges we face. Second, we come together to carry one another's burdens (Galatians 6:2). It is worthy of deep thought that God has chosen this unique group of people to be together this year to support one another and to lighten each other's load. This is especially profound when we consider that some in your group will be hard for you to love at times and may bring uniquely heavy burdens. Third, we are called to teach one another (Colossians 3:16). Humans are social creatures. Generally, we learn best in groups because others bring their unique perspectives and experiences and share them with us. God reminds us in his Word that we are called to teach one another (Colossians 3:16), even when we feel we have nothing to offer or nothing to learn. Finally, God brings us together because he wants us to go deep. What does this mean? God commands us to confess our sins to one another (James 5:16). In the same way that Adam and Eve hid from God in the Garden (Genesis 3:8), we tend to hide in our shame as well. We make all sorts of leaf coverings that do not work. They simply reveal that we have something to hide. Your Fellows year may be the first time in your life that you are truly vulnerable with others.

  These are just four aspects of life in a Fellows community. The weekly Roundtable is designed to be a time for you to do some of this important work. We sometimes think that being vulnerable requires bravery. While that is not entirely wrong, it is more accurate to say that being truly vulnerable in community requires faith. It requires trust that God is with us as we reveal those things that have otherwise remained hidden in our hearts.

In general, Roundtable will be fun and easy. However, there will be times that are challenging as well. As people express themselves, you might find some of the conversations to be awkward, confusing, or frustrating. Roundtable might delve into difficult parts of your story. For this gathering time to work, everyone must be present and trying. As you enter difficult discussions, it may be tempting to withdraw physically or emotionally. In those moments, please do not underestimate the impact of your absence. Your thoughts and experiences are important because only you can share them. Genuine community requires you to be present as an active participant. Roundtable done well requires you to be vulnerable. You may find it helpful to prepare for Roundtable each week by considering your tendencies in group discussions. Do you tend to dominate? Perhaps you withdraw from challenging conversations. Are you someone who expects others to pursue you as a test of friendship? Do you try to be the wise and knowing sage in a group? Maybe you tend to be judgmental. To be a truly active participant in an intentional community requires honest reflection on your own style and preferences in a group.

Each Fellows program has its own Roundtable traditions. Generally, they all share the same core elements: a meal together, worship time, discussion on a topic, and prayer. This book is a guide for the discussions.

Our challenge to you as a Fellows cohort, is to integrate the other elements so that each Roundtable is cohesive. For example, you might select worship songs and readings that are tied to the discussion topic for the week. You will find that this approach prevents Roundtable from seeming random. Threading the discussion topic through the other elements of Roundtable will also help make Roundtable easier to manage and plan each week. It is important to remember that this book is just a starting point for your discussions. We encourage you to continue the conversations on these topics throughout the week, in class, and with your host families and mentors. The chapters in this book can only go so deep. It is up to you to take the learning to the next level by delving deeper into God's Word and by keeping the conversation going.

You are a unique cohort, brought together by God for this season. You are different from every Fellows class that came before you and everyone that will come after you. Because you are a unique group, your Roundtable experience will also be unique. Embrace this uniqueness! Enjoy one another. Make this time your own. Under the guidance of your Fellows program leaders, keep the traditions and make some new ones. The goal of Roundtable is not to grow in knowledge alone, but also in life. This is a unique moment to grow in Christ with this group of people, learning together, forming a community, and preparing for the future. Welcome to Roundtable!

# Introduction

## USING THIS BOOK

This book is designed to be a conversation starter and a weekly reader. It is meant to get you thinking and talking. While it is primarily for TFI Fellows communities, it could also be used by program alumni and other small groups. The book has four sections: Vocation, Service, Community, and Leadership. It is not trying to cover all subjects in depth; instead, it serves as a discussion guide, to be read slowly over time — just one chapter per week. Therefore, if you read it straight through rather than week by week, you might find it somewhat choppy.

This book is intended to fit into the larger structure of your Fellows program. Your program should engage you in a deep, comprehensive study of God's Word, helping you develop and deepen your Christian worldview through which you see all aspects of life, with Christ at the center of it all. Your Fellows program should equip you in the practical aspects of work, servanthood, church life, community life, and personal discipleship. This book is meant to accompany these other program elements, not to supplant them. With that in mind, receive and use this book for what it is — a conversation starter for the weekly Roundtable gathering.

To get the most out of Roundtable, read the assigned chapter *before* attending Roundtable each week. Make notes and write down your questions and thoughts. Read through and meditate on the Bible readings for the week. Come prepared to discuss the questions at the end of each chapter. Your program leader may give you additional readings and may have additional questions to aid good discussion.

SECTION 1

# VOCATION

Our study begins with vocation. The word vocation is synonymous with *calling* and comes from the Latin word *vocare*, which is also the root of the word *voice*. *Vocare* means *to call* or *invoke*.

Right from the start, we can see that vocation is relational. God calls us and we respond. He is the caller, and we are the called. Understood this way, the word vocation speaks to something about God and about us. He is an inviting God, calling us to be part of what he is doing. He is not distant but close enough to call and to be with us as we pursue our callings. It is in him that we live, move, and have our being (Acts 17:28). It is an ongoing relationship.

God's calling upon us is not just about our jobs, although that is the most common application of the word vocation. God has transcendent callings on our lives as well — to love, think, serve, and lead. We will explore each of these in the chapters to come. Remember, this book is meant to be a conversation starter. There is much more to be said than what is contained in these pages. Let this section on vocation be a starting place for you and your Fellows class as you explore the topic of vocation throughout your life.

# 1

## CALLED TO FOLLOW

Jesus is Lord. This statement is arguably the best, most profound truth in the universe. He is Lord over all Creation, which means all things, all ideas, and all people. This beautiful truth has significant implications. He reigns over all of life and every part of life. There is no hidden part that he does not see. Apart from our sins, there is no part of us that he does not love. As we start the Fellows year and come together for Roundtable, there is no better place to start than with the person of Jesus Christ.

As we reflect on this truth, we should be struck by the power and majesty of Jesus. By his hand all things were made. He sustains all things (Colossians 1:15-17). And as he works to set Creation right, it is by his hand and his blood, that he is making all things new. Scripture depicts Jesus as the mighty King of Kings and Prince of Peace. He is the Great High Priest and Great Shepherd of the Sheep. When Moses was told to say, "I AM has sent me to you" (Exodus 3:14), this statement was about Jesus, the second person of the Trinity who makes the I AM claims in John 6-15. In making these bold statements, Jesus was declaring himself to be the God of the Old Testament, the Creator

God. In John's vision of the throne in heaven, Jesus says, "Behold, I am making all things new" (Revelation 21:5). From this heavenly position, he quotes the prophet Isaiah (Isaiah 43:19) and again identifies himself as the God of Israel.

This realization, that Jesus Christ is the eternal God, is a staggering and beautiful truth. Upon realizing whom he was seeing as he stood before the risen Christ, the disciple Thomas declared in awe, "My Lord and my God!" (John 20:28). We, too, as we think about Jesus, should be awestruck. But we can easily lose sight of this truth and its implications. In seasons of spiritual dryness, when we have become bored with Jesus, this amazing, awe-inspiring truth slips from its rightful place in our minds.

Professor Vincent Bacote of Wheaton College offers a helpful way to think about Jesus as our teacher and ourselves as his followers: "A disciple of Jesus is more than a convert, but a true, committed follower. A disciple is someone who is following their teacher, not as a kind of fan. You are taking on what the teacher is teaching, becoming another image, so to speak, of your rabbi."[1]

The person of Jesus Christ should be the driving force of our every thought and action. The Apostle Paul challenges us in this regard to "take every thought captive

---

1. Vincent Bacote, *The Political Disciple: A Theology of Public Life*. Leadership lecture given at Eastbrook Church in Milwaukee, WI, September 28, 2020.

for Christ" (II Corinthians 10:5). To pursue this inward and outward commitment and personal transformation is what it means to be a follower of Christ.

Jesus is the God of history. By that we mean that he is unfolding history like a story right before our eyes. Unlike many stories, this is not a fanciful tale set in a make-believe land. It could not be more real to us because we are part of it! He has given each of us a role in the unfolding story of human history. By God's sovereign design, our lives matter because he knows us and has made a place for us in his real-life story. Scripture reveals that God's unfolding history has four distinct parts: Creation, Fall, Redemption, and Consummation. The first three parts of this history have already happened. In Genesis, we learn of God's *Creation* of all things. We also learn about the *Fall* of humanity, the result of human sin against God. The Old Testament anticipates the coming Messiah, who finally arrives in the person of Jesus in the gospel accounts of the New Testament. Jesus brought *Redemption*. In the coming final season, *Consummation*, Jesus will return and complete his work by making all things new (Revelation 21:5). Some have described God's history in progress as a four-act play.[2] Others refer to it as the *Four-Chapter*

---

2. Tim Challies and Josh Byers, *Visual Theology: Seeing and Understanding the Truth about God* (Grand Rapids: Zondervan Academic, 2016).

Gospel.[3,4,5] (*Note*: We will use the term Four-Chapter Gospel in this book.) It should be no surprise to learn that Jesus is Lord over every one of the four chapters! Scripture depicts this clearly. Consider the first chapter of the Four-Chapter Gospel, Creation. We learn in John 1, Colossians 1, and Hebrews 1 that Jesus is the one through whom all things were made. The earth is his and all that is in it (Psalm 24:1). He made human beings, man and woman, and placed us here to be part of his creative work. Through these creative activities, we get a glimpse of God's character and power. He is a designer, planner, and worker. He is an inviting God who designed us to be part of what he is doing in this world. He is a relational God who cares about our well-being.

In chapter two of God's Four-Chapter Gospel, the Fall, we see God as both Judge and Savior. He sees our sin and the way we hide in our shame, and yet he pursues us. He makes a righteous judgment over our rebellion and makes a way for redemption (Genesis 3). In chapter three of the unfolding story, Redemption, Jesus appears in the flesh. He comes to us fully God and fully man, the one and

---

3. Craig G. Bartholomew and Michael W. Goheen, *The True Story of the Whole World: Finding Your Place in the Biblical Drama* (Grand Rapids: Faith Alive, 2009).

4. Philip Graham Ryken, *Christian Worldview: A Student's Guide* (Wheaton: Crossway, 2013).

5. Hugh Whelchel, *All Things New: Rediscovering the Four-Chapter Gospel* (McLean: The Institute for Faith Work and Economics, 2016).

only *God-man*. Through his life, death, and resurrection, he provides the way for us to be restored. On a personal level, Jesus is revealed in the story as our Savior, in whom we can put our trust. More broadly, Jesus is also revealed as the Conquering King who has come to put an end to evil and rebellion, and to bring lasting peace and justice on a cosmic scale. Finally, in the chapter to come, Consummation, Jesus promises to make all things new (Revelation 21:5), establishing the New Heavens and the New Earth, in which we will live and work and enjoy God forever. Throughout this Four-Chapter Gospel, Jesus is not only present but in control. At each step, even though we stray from him time and again, he remains faithful and on mission.

Without a full understanding of Jesus as he is depicted in Scripture, it is easy to limit him in our thought life and elsewhere. For example, we might divide our life into compartments with labels such as "church life" and "work life." Sometimes it is helpful to make these divisions to keep the various aspects of our lives from overtaking each other. But when we consciously or unconsciously divide our life into a part that is for Jesus and a part that is not for Jesus, we have a problem. We have fallen into what has been called the Sunday-Monday Divide. We might be one person at church and quite a different person at work, to the point that our friends at church might not recognize our work self, and our colleagues at work might not recognize our church self. Our career aspirations and motivations can be fueled by worldly ideals and ambitions rather than Kingdom ideals and ambitions. This double life is common among Christians, young and old. The good news is that Jesus himself is the remedy to the divided life. With an understanding of who he truly is, Lord of all and Lord of every aspect of life, movement toward a cohesive life in Christ is possible, by his grace. He is the Great Shepherd of the Sheep and will pursue you in love and without fail.

In addition to being Lord over all, Jesus is Immanuel, God with us. He is with us in the sense that he has a physical body, fully God and fully human. He is incarnate. He is also with us in the sense that he gets us. He understands us. He was tempted in every way (Hebrews 4:15) and understands what it is to be human — frail and subject to sickness and death. Unlike us, however, he was without sin. He lived the perfect life and died the perfect death — the new and better Adam (Romans 5:18-19). Jesus, as one of us, did what the first Adam, and indeed the rest of us, could not do. Jesus, Immanuel, is not a distant God. He is a close and personal God who knows what it is to be human, and therefore can be the perfect Great High Priest (Hebrews 2:17), standing in the gap for us. He worked with his hands. He walked and ate with his friends. He cried, mourned, and suffered.

This is where we begin our Fellows journey, meditating on the person of Jesus Christ and reflecting on the idea that we are called to follow him. It is a fitting place to start since he is, after all, the Alpha and Omega, the Beginning and End (Revelation 22:13). As Christians, we are called to live for him. But what does that mean in practice? First, it means that the most reasonable and rational approach to living is to build one's life upon the foundation of Jesus Christ, guided by his Word. Second, it means that we have the assurance of a cohesive life that is held together by Christ, even though we experience it in parts and seasons. To us, our work life can seem disconnected from our home life and church life. Our practical aspirations can seem out of sync with our spiritual longings. Our transition from the relative freedom of youth and college life to the responsibilities of adulthood can seem loaded with peril. But we have assurance because in Christ all things hold together. The One through whom all things were made is at the center of our lives. In him, life is neither random nor scattered but meaningful because we find ourselves in him and his unfolding story.

As we close out this first chapter, there is an important point to consider. If you are a follower of Christ, born again, redeemed by his blood, you have nothing to fear (Romans 8:15). Your eternal life in Christ has already begun, and he holds you fast in the faith he has given to you as a gift (Ephesians 2:8). Throughout this study, we will explore many aspects of the Christian life — vocation, our call to serve and lead, and various aspects of life in community. As you work through these topics, remember that you already belong to Jesus. You do not need to earn his love. You have it in full. In our work or service, we are not trying to earn a place in his heart. Instead, our work or service provides opportunities to worship him by reflecting his glory and by honoring his good design and desires for us. Our work and service are also ways to bring flourishing into the world. Step into these studies embracing the great freedom you have in Christ.

## SCRIPTURE READINGS

In the beginning was the Word, and the Word was with God, and the Word was God. He was in the beginning with God. All things were made through him, and without him was not anything made that was made. In him was life, and the life was the light of men. The light shines in the darkness, and the darkness has not overcome it. – John 1:1-5

Your father Abraham rejoiced that he would see my day. He saw it and was glad. So the Jews said to him, "You are not yet fifty years old, and have you seen Abraham?" Jesus said to them, "Truly, truly, I say to you, before Abraham was, I am." – John 8:56-58

He is the image of the invisible God, the firstborn of all creation. For by him all things were created, in heaven and on earth, visible and invisible, whether thrones or dominions or rulers or authorities — all things were created through him and for him. And he is before all things, and in him all things hold together. – Colossians 1:15-17

Long ago, at many times and in many ways, God spoke to our fathers by the prophets, but in these last days he has spoken to us by his Son, whom he appointed the heir of all things, through whom also he created the world. He is the radiance of the glory of God and the exact imprint of his nature, and he upholds the universe by the word of his power. After making purification for sins, he sat down at the right hand of the Majesty on high, having become as much superior to angels as the name he has inherited is more excellent than theirs. – Hebrews 1:1-4

And he who was seated on the throne said, "Behold, I am making all things new." Also he said, "Write this down, for these words are trustworthy and true." – Revelation 21:5

## DISCUSSION QUESTIONS

1. Was Christ central in your home growing up? Was he "present" in your family conversations and activities? Would you say that your parents modeled a life lived with Christ at the center of all things? How has this aspect of your childhood influenced you today?

2. Talk about your experience of knowing Christ as "Lord over all" and "Lord over all of me." Do you find it easier to see him as one or the other?

3. In what ways do you find joy and comfort in the image of Christ as it is discussed in this chapter?

4. As you read through the scripture passages for this chapter, what stuck out as particularly relevant to you and this moment in your life?

5. Have you struggled with the double life, as many Christians do? What has been your experience with this? How do you hope to grow in this area during your Fellows year?

6. Is there anything that scares you about giving yourself fully to Christ and living fully for him? For example, does it worry you that your non-Christian friends might think differently of you if you lived your life openly with Christ at the center?

7. What are some of the ways Christians marginalize Christ in our lives? What are some ways that you do this personally?

8. As you think about ways to lead others, what are some ways to share these ideas about who Christ is with your Christian friends that do not have a complete picture of him, and your friends that do not claim Christ as their Lord and Savior?

9. As you begin this Fellows year, what are some things you and your group can do to keep Jesus, in all his glory, front and center in your lives and in your Fellows experience?

# 2

# CALLED TO LOVE

The call to love is clear and repeated throughout the Bible. What has come to be known as The Greatest Commandment is that we love God with all our heart, soul, and mind, and that we love our neighbor as ourselves (Matthew 22:37-40). In giving us this command, Jesus was quoting the *Shema* (Deuteronomy 6:4), the Old Testament requirement to love God with our whole being and to love others as we love ourselves (Leviticus 19:18). Jesus not only invites us to love one another but commands it. In making this command, he says something about how we are to treat one another, but he also says something about himself. "A new commandment I give to you, that you love one another: just as I have loved you, you also are to love one another. By this, all people will know that you are my disciples if you have love for one another" (John 13:34-35).

The first thing to ask ourselves as we read this verse is, "Who makes commandments?" Only God! In making this commandment, Jesus is telling his disciples, and us, who he really is. Second, he sets the standard for love. In his book, *Biblical Critical Theory*, Chris Watkin writes, "Love is the epicenter of the distinctly Christian way of being in the world – not power, respect, or tolerance, and not equality, justice, freedom, enlightenment, or submission .... Love is to be the signature disposition of Christ's disciples."[1] How are we to love one another? The answer is that we are to love one another as Christ has loved us — sacrificially, humbly, and with great intention and faithful pursuit. In addition to the love itself, we also know that it is by our love for one another that the world will recognize us as his followers. It is meant to be our brand or trademark.

What does it mean to love as Christ loved? With this commandment and the many calls in scripture to love, we need to become life-long students of love. We need to continually educate ourselves in the concept and practice of love, which really means becoming students of God's character. Fortunately, scripture offers a lot of direction about how we can do that. We are to love earnestly (I Peter 4:8), that is, with genuineness and not just outward appearance. We are to love with brotherly affection (Romans 12:10) and tenderheartedness (Ephesians 4:32), which we can understand to mean empathy and warmth. We are to love not in words alone but in deed and in truth (I John 3:18). We might say that Christian love is not just a warm sentiment toward another person. Instead, love is action-oriented and intended to increase the flourishing of

---

1. Chris Watkin, *Biblical Critical Theory: How the Bible's Unfolding Story Makes Sense of Modern Life and Culture* (Grand Rapids: Zondervan Academic, 2022), 390.

that person. And ultimately, we are called to love sacrificially (John 15:13; Romans 12:1-2). This is the highest challenge of true Christian love. Jesus calls us to love as he did, giving his life so that others might have life. Similarly, he calls us to be living sacrifices, taking up our crosses in such a way that others might flourish.

What is love? As we endeavor to love in thought, word, and deed, we should be clear about what love is and what it is not. I Corinthians 13 is often called The Love Chapter of the Bible. In remarkably plain language, the Apostle Paul outlines a godly definition of love. In verses 4-6, he offers a succinct definition of love that we should memorize: "Love is patient and kind; love does not envy or boast; it is not arrogant or rude. It does not insist on its own way; it is not irritable or resentful; it does not rejoice at wrong-doing but rejoices with the truth."

Patience and kindness are at the heart of love, as we bear with one another in our shortcomings and frailties. From these two positives, Paul switches to a list of negatives, things that love is not: envious, boastful, arrogant, rude, irritable, or resentful. A key element of this passage, one that conveys a lot about God's design for human love and often one with which we struggle the most, is that love does not demand its own way. Have you stopped to consider the ways that you demand your own way? This passage may conjure up images of a child stomping his feet in a tantrum as an attempt to get his parents to bend to his will. The reality is that by the time we reach adulthood, we have become very good at demanding our way through various methods, not just stomping our feet. If we are honest with ourselves, we must admit that we demand our way in much more sophisticated, subtle, and even manipulative ways in relationships, at home, and at work.

Finally, Paul indicates that there is a moral standard for love: it does not rejoice at wrongdoing but rejoices with the truth. For example, love is never about retaliation or getting even because we are not called to be people of vengeance (Romans 12:19). In romantic relationships, love is not promiscuous but is ever faithful. In these and other ways, the world has tried to redefine love over the centuries but the enduring standard for love is God's character alone because he is love (I John 4:16). God is not subject to any higher laws or definitions of love. True love is defined by who he is. God is love, and we are called to bear his image. His Word is our guide to how God wants us to love him and each other.

Before thinking about love in specific relationships, let us think about it in a broad sense. What does it mean that we are called to love and to be recognized by the way we love? Dr. Steve Garber, in his book *Visions of Vocation*, challenges us to look at the world with clear eyes.[2] Specifically, he challenges us to look at the broken world with love, despite its corruption and rebellion against God. He is not saying that we should remain idle about injustice or look upon sin with approval. He is saying that we should look at the people of the world, who are sinners just like us,

---

2. Steven Garber, *Visions of Vocation: Common Grace for the Common Good* (Downer's Grove: Intervarsity Press, 2014).

with love and compassion. This is how God looks at us after all. He loves us even though our sin is an abomination to him (Psalm 51:4; Colossians 3:5-6). He loves us and is merciful to us, even as he calls us out of our sin. Applying this to the workplace, imagine what it would be like to love your colleagues, even the most difficult ones. In *Visions of Vocation*, Dr. Garber tells us that our vocation is integral, not incidental to the *missio Dei*, the mission of God.[3] If we consider that God is love and that he loves the world (John 3:16), then our only conclusion is that our work necessarily involves loving those we encounter in our workplace — colleagues, supervisors, shareholders, and clients. What about the world of politics? Even in the public square where people are deeply divided and vitriolic toward one another, we are called to love. Those across the aisle from us are not enemies as much as they are simply people with whom we disagree. They are human beings with dignity, made in God's image. Again, we are called to love even those with whom we have deep disagreements. The

---

3. What is the mission of God or *missio Dei?* From the beginning, God has been making a people for himself who know and worship him. In his mission is the promise that he will be our God and we will be his people (Genesis 17:8; Exodus 29:45). He created a place for us to live and worship him. He provides a way for us to "fill the earth." When we rebel against him, he provides a means of redemption through his son. And he makes a covenantal promise to make all things new when Christ returns. A key idea of God's design in the *missio Dei* is that God does some of his work through his people. We are not just watching history go by. We are part of it. He invites us to be part of his work. This is the relationship between our vocation and his mission.

workplace and public square are just two examples that demonstrate that we are called to love broadly in every sphere of life — in our families, neighborhoods, churches, and workplaces.

As students of love, we cannot focus on the *concept* of love alone. We are called to *practice* love. We are called to love real people in real circumstances. We are called to love the individuals God has brought into our lives — family, friends, and acquaintances. In the messiness of life and relationships, there are always those in our lives that are hard to love. What makes someone hard to love? We can think about this by inverting the definition of love in I Corinthians 13:4-6. Those that are hard to love are those that are not patient or kind. Do you know people who are envious, boastful, arrogant, or rude? Maybe they are irritable, resentful, malicious, or untruthful. Perhaps they try to convince you or others that wrongdoing is OK or that bending the truth is acceptable. There is a very good chance you have people with these traits in your life. What is more, these people are rarely able to recognize these attitudes and behaviors in themselves. How can we serve and lead friends and relatives that are hard to love? On one hand, we are called to be patient and long-suffering, understanding that no one is perfect. On the other, we are called to teach one another (Colossians 3:16). One of the most difficult things we can do in our closest relationships is to confront unloving attitudes and behaviors. It requires a lot of trust on the part of the recipient and a lot of gentleness on the part of the confronter. During your Fellows year, you will almost certainly have opportunities to practice both skills — trust and gentleness. This is an intentional aspect of the program and its intimate cohort design.

As we grow in servant leadership, a challenge for us is to become skilled at speaking the truth in love and speaking love in the truth. We tend to favor one over the other rather than holding them together. Fortunately, God has not left us to wander and figure everything out on our own. He has given us his Word, eternal wisdom from our loving Creator. It is our only guide to love and truth.

As we consider the reality that some people are hard to love, we must be open to the idea that we are also hard to love, at least sometimes. Have you taken time to confront your own attitudes and behaviors in this regard? We all have blind spots. Like the back of our own head, blind spots are impossible to see without help, without mirrors. To honestly assess our attitudes and behaviors, it is imperative that we have friends and family to help us. It can be uncomfortable and unsettling at times, but being vulnerable in this way is one of the keys to spiritual growth. Have you invited friends and family to help you see your blind spots? If no one is walking with you in this way, is it possible that the people in your life do not feel invited? What are some ways that you are hard to love by the definition of love in I Corinthians 13? Perhaps there are times that you are not patient or kind. Perhaps you are envious of others, boastful, arrogant, or even rude. Are you someone who separates truth and love to make a point or to promote worldly values and attitudes that are not consistent with God's Word? If we are honest with ourselves, we all do some of these things some of the time. As you consider these shortcomings, remember that God loves you while he calls you out of your sins. Jesus has already paid the price for them and is making a place for you. You do not need to perfect your love before coming to Jesus because he is already there with you. As his image-bearer, he calls you to love because it reflects who he is. He is patient and kind with you as you grow. So, come and take on his yoke.

## SCRIPTURE READINGS

And he said to him, "You shall love the Lord your God with all your heart and with all your soul and with all your mind. This is the great and first commandment. And a second is like it: You shall love your neighbor as yourself. On these two commandments depend all the Law and the Prophets." – Matthew 22:37-40

A new commandment I give to you, that you love one another: just as I have loved you, you also are to love one another. By this all people will know that you are my disciples, if you have love for one another. – John 13:34-35

Greater love has no one than this, that someone lay down his life for his friends. – John 15:13

Love one another with brotherly affection. Outdo one another in showing honor. –Romans 12:10

Love is patient and kind; love does not envy or boast; it is not arrogant or rude. It does not insist on its own way; it is not irritable or resentful; it does not rejoice at wrongdoing but rejoices with the truth. – I Corinthians 13:4-6

Above all, keep loving one another earnestly, since love covers a multitude of sins. – I Peter 4:8

So we have come to know and to believe the love that God has for us. God is love, and whoever abides in love abides in God, and God abides in him. – I John 4:16

## DISCUSSION QUESTIONS

1. What are some of the most memorable acts of love you have personally witnessed in your life?

2. What are some of the ways that people in your life love you the best?

3. As a group, come up with a good, biblically-sound working definition of love. How do you think your family, friends, church, and others would receive this definition?

4. On a scale of 1-10, are you hard or easy to love? Explain.

5. What are some ways people have failed to love you in your life? What are some of the ways you have failed to love them?

6. What would it mean to love the hardest-to-love people in your life? In other words, what would be required of you to truly love them?

7. Would you say that love, as defined in the Bible, is consistent with the world's definition of love? In what ways are they the same? In what ways do they differ?

8. To the extent that the world's concept of love differs from the biblical idea of love, what role do Christians play in that tension? How can we stand on and for truth while also maintaining friendships and relationships with those opposed to the Gospel?

9. How can we love in the workplace, at church, and in society in a way that is genuine, God-honoring, and not confined and defined by the world's ideas of how it wants to be loved?

# 3

# CALLED TO THINK

Scripture is filled with commands and calls to engage our minds. Based on the small sampling of passages at the end of this chapter, God clearly cares about how we think and what we think about. He cares that our thoughts are actively aligned with his design and desires. He cares that we are not caught up in worldly thinking. In fact, the Apostle Paul calls us to no longer be conformed to the pattern of the world but to be transformed by the renewing of our minds (Romans 12:2). In giving such a command, Paul is first acknowledging that we are, by default, conformed to the world's pattern of thinking. Given that worldly thinking is our default, breaking out of it will require significant and sustained effort. It will require a commitment to studying and applying the Bible to everyday life. It will require proactively challenging the ideological and philosophical norms of the world by evaluating them against the standard of God's character and design for us as his image-bearers. As we consider the weightiness of this command, the good news is that God loves us. He knows we are frail and apt to sin. So, while this command is a real and important aspect of the

Christian life, we can know that we are not trying to earn our way into heaven by having all our thoughts aligned with the Lord in advance. In sanctifying us, the Holy Spirit is working in our hearts and minds to transform them by God's Word.

Harry Blamires, an Anglican theologian, and student of C. S. Lewis wrote a book called *The Christian Mind*. In it, he writes, "There is nothing in our experience, however trivial, worldly, or even evil, which cannot be thought about Christianly. There is likewise nothing in our experience, however sacred, which cannot be thought about secularly."[1] When we read that we should transform our minds by turning away from worldly thinking, we might be tempted to think that Paul is calling us to think only about Christian topics all the time: church, corporate worship, and so on. He is not. He is challenging us to work in conjunction with the Holy Spirit to form a new view of the world, a new *worldview*, a Christian worldview. He is calling us to adopt and deploy that worldview in every area of life — at home, at church, at work, in the public square, in our inner thought lives — everywhere. We are called to a worldview framed by the foundational idea that Jesus is at the center of it all.

Christians are called to be thoughtful people who are not simply dancing through life, oblivious to the world of ideas around them. The Christian faith is a whole-

---

1. Harry Blamires, *The Christian Mind: How Should a Christian Think?* (Vancouver: Regent College Publishing, 2005), 45.

person faith. That is, it is not simply an emotive faith of song and prayerful meditation. While those are important aspects of the Christian life, Christianity is just as much about what and how we think and how we apply our intellect to real life. In Romans 1, Paul tells us that the world has become futile in its thinking. Why would he say this? He says it because the world has lost sight of God and its dependence on him. In Romans 8, he tells us that Christians (i.e., those in the Spirit) set their minds on things above. In his second letter, the Apostle Peter picks up these themes and charges us to prepare our minds for action (I Peter 1:13). What an exciting adventure! God is inviting us into the truth by giving us his Word and his Spirit, so that we may be transformed in every way — including the transformation of our minds. So, let us go forward into lives of active thinking and active consideration of the world's ideas and philosophies always viewing them in the light of scripture.

One aspect of our call to think stems from our call to co-create with God. In the account of God's Creation, God commands us to fill the earth and to make something of it (Genesis 1:28). Some theologians refer to this command as the *Cultural Mandate*. He established us as caretakers of this world (Genesis 2:15) and as co-creators of a God-honoring society. Sometimes, we think creativity is reserved for a special few — artists, writers, and musicians. In much of its recent advertising, Apple Corporation describes its products as being for so-called "Creatives." When we hear a term like that, we might think, "Oh, that's not me." We might think of "Creatives" as graphic artists, filmmakers, photographers, or game designers. Apple products are useful for all sorts of creative work: spreadsheets, email, texting, managing a calendar, organizing a project. Sometimes we think of these activities as ordinary or boring, rather than creative. However, creating and updating a spreadsheet requires a tremendous amount of creativity. The same is true of a well-crafted email.

When we understand that God is present with us (Matthew 28:20) in everything we do and that we are called to do everything as unto the Lord (Colossians 3:23), we can see that nothing we do or think is ordinary or boring. Those are labels applied by a Godless worldview and an untransformed mind. When we recognize and celebrate the presence of God as we do ordinary things, and as we work for his glory in all things, we are transforming our minds. We are abandoning the worldly idea that God is, at best, a distant God who cares little for ordinary human life. And as we allow ourselves to get excited about these concepts, we are well on our way to "thinking Christianly" about all things; we are well on our way toward enjoying one of the freedoms we have in Christ: the freedom to enjoy the ever-present God in real and ordinary things.

Decision-making is another important form of thinking. To decide is to think. And yet, we can sometimes waffle in our thoughts about God and what is true. We can wallow in indecision about matters of faith and other important things. As those called by God to think, and to be aligned with God in our thoughts, we are also called away from indecision. James 1:8 says that the one who doubts God, meaning the one who cannot make up his mind, is double-minded and unstable. While we are called to love and show grace to those who are wrestling with doubts, we are also called to be wise by not following them, not sitting under their teaching, and not getting caught in the pattern of indecision ourselves. We are to work toward a surety of faith so that we might lead others. I Kings 18 recounts a story in which Elijah charges the people to overcome their indecision about God. Verse 21 says, "How long will you go limping between two different opinions? If the Lord is God, follow him; but if Baal, then follow him." The Apostle Paul writes in II Corinthians 10:5, "We destroy arguments and every lofty opinion raised against the knowledge of God and take every thought captive to obey Christ." In II Peter 1:10, Peter charges us to "make our calling and election *sure*." These are not words of indecision but of commitment. If we stop and think about the idea of decision-making and God's call for us to be firm in our faith and knowledge of him, we can conclude that decision-making is a key capability given to us by God for the work of the Cultural Mandate.

To glorify God by filling the earth and making something of it will require a lot of good, careful, decisive thought and action. He has equipped us with the ability to decide ordinary and extraordinary things. This line of thinking shows us something truly remarkable about God and his relationship to us. God is the Almighty One, sovereign over everything (Isaiah 45:7-9). And yet, he gives us the ability, and even the requirement, to decide things. In other words, he is sovereign and yet we are not puppets. Seen this way, we can understand that our decisions in no way detract from his sovereign power. Instead, they magnify it. From our perspective, it can seem that either he is sovereign, or we are. Either he makes real decisions, or we do. In making godly, scripture-guided decisions, we bring honor to God by showing that he is *so* powerful that even our human conception of sovereignty is not big enough for him. He *is* sovereign, and we *are not* puppets.

It is easy to get off track in our thinking. That is why scripture so frequently addresses the call to think. We need these reminders to help us stay in alignment with his call on us. There are many ways that we lose sight of God's call to think. As you prepare for discussion on this chapter, consider these three:

1. *We sometimes forget that God's way is true, right, and beautiful.* We can be fooled by the world's ideas about God and ourselves; fooled into thinking that scripture misleads us or is no longer relevant in the modern world. As a result, we can fail to equip ourselves with God's Word and instead adopt worldly ideas and values. These patterns are not new. They have been happening since Adam and Eve rebelled against God.

2. *We forget that we are never alone with our thoughts.* It may seem that thoughts are private and confined to one's mind. The reality is that God knows it all. A helpful prayer in the Book of Common Prayer says, "Almighty God, to you all hearts are open, all desires known, and from you no secrets are hid. Cleanse the thoughts of our hearts by the inspiration of your Holy Spirit, that we may perfectly love you and worthily magnify your

holy name, through Christ, our Lord. Amen."[2] In Hebrews 4:12-13, we learn that scripture discerns the "thoughts and intentions of the heart" and that "no creature is hidden from his sight." It is not only God who can see our thoughts and emotions. Our outward behavior often reveals to others that something is going on in there. Observant friends and family can often see into our inner world of thoughts, motivations, and intentions. By imagining that our thoughts are known only to us, we can be drawn into loneliness or self-pity by mistakenly believing that no one could possibly understand us or that we are the only one who struggles.

3. *We forget that we are Ambassadors who are called to represent the whole story of Jesus to the world.* We are not here simply to be saved and to wait for eternal life with Christ. Yes, we await a wonderful future in him. But we are also on a mission now: to make Christ known to everyone and to show his love to the world. Making him known does not mean that we are called to share the salvation message while leaving out the rest of God's design for the world. No, we are called to share the *entire* message of Christ, including his character and good design and desires for human beings.

---

2. Collect for Purity. *The Book of Common Prayer.* The Church Pension Fund, 1928, 65.

As you consider the call to think, you may have the impression that God is calling you to a small world of thought limited to a set of ideas called Christianity. The reality is just the opposite. The Christian faith opens the door to every good thought. The only limitation on good thinking is the kind of thinking that denies God, the story of scripture, or God's design for humanity. Otherwise, every topic is open for godly consideration — work, family, education, sex, science, art, music, economics, literature, technology, politics — everything. Seen this way, the Christian is truly free in Christ to explore a limitless world of ideas and thoughts. What an adventure! The infinite God is inviting you to explore these concepts with him for all eternity.

## SCRIPTURE READINGS

"Come now, let us reason together," says the Lord. "Though your sins are like scarlet, they shall be as white as snow; though they are red like crimson, they shall become like wool." – Isaiah 1:18

Go to the ant, O sluggard; consider her ways, and be wise. – Proverbs 6:6

But I say to you that everyone who looks at a woman with lustful intent has already committed adultery with her in his heart. – Matthew 5:28

# Called to Think

And why are you anxious about clothing? Consider the lilies of the field, how they grow: they neither toil nor spin, yet I tell you, even Solomon in all his glory was not arrayed like one of these. – Matthew 6:28

The apostles and the elders were gathered together to consider this matter. – Acts 15:6

For although they knew God, they did not honor him as God or give thanks to him, but they became futile in their thinking, and their foolish hearts were darkened. – Romans 1:21

For those who live according to the flesh set their minds on the things of the flesh, but those who live according to the Spirit set their minds on the things of the Spirit. For to set the mind on the flesh is death, but to set the mind on the Spirit is life and peace. – Romans 8:5-6

Do not be conformed to this world, but be transformed by the renewal of your mind, that by testing you may discern what is the will of God, what is good and acceptable and perfect. For by the grace given to me I say to everyone among you not to think of himself more highly than he ought to think, but to think with sober judgment, each according to the measure of faith that God has assigned. – Romans 12:2-3

Brothers, do not be children in your thinking. Be infants in evil, but in your thinking be mature. – 1 Corinthians 14:20

Therefore do not be foolish, but understand what the will of the Lord is. – Ephesians 5:17

Finally, brothers, whatever is true, whatever is honorable, whatever is just, whatever is pure, whatever is lovely, whatever is commendable, if there is any excellence, if there is anything worthy of praise, think about these things. What you have learned and received and heard and seen in me — practice these things, and the God of peace will be with you. –Philippians 4:8-9

Set your minds on things that are above, not on things that are on earth. – Colossians 3:2

And let us consider how to stir up one another to love and good works – Hebrews 10:24

Therefore, preparing your minds for action, and being sober-minded, set your hope fully on the grace that will be brought to you at the revelation of Jesus Christ. – I Peter 1:13

## DISCUSSION QUESTIONS

1. Paul and other writers of scripture have little love for the "wisdom" of the world. There is also evidence that the world often has little love for the wisdom of the Bible. Where are these worldviews most at odds in the world today?

2. In Romans 12:2, the Apostle Paul commands us to "no longer conform to the pattern of the world, but to be transformed by the renewing of our minds." The passage suggests that we already are conformed to the pattern of the world and that we need to change. What are some ways that Christians adopt and promote worldly ideas and values rather than biblical ideas and values?

3. Scripture is clear that God is sovereign. It is also clear that we are responsible for our thoughts and decisions. How does this idea sit with you: God is sovereign over everything and yet he has designed us to think real thoughts and make real decisions? How does this truth impact your sense of his power…and yours?

4. When you think about being an ambassador of Christ, with the mission of promoting Christ's love and design for the world, what does that mean to you? What is most exciting and/or most daunting about this aspect of our calling as Christians?

5. Consider the wide range of things we can think about: the arts, science, law, education, social structures, politics, electric vehicles, technology, social media, the environment, etc. Some Christians compartmentalize these and other topics, separating them into "spiritual" and "secular" realms. This separation can often lead to the "double life" in which a Christian's spiritual life and secular lives are separate and distinct. How can

we, as Christians, integrate our thoughts into a single, Christ-centered, cohesive whole?

6. What are some ways that your closest Christian friends can encourage you as you seek to think differently, transformed by scripture?

# 4

# CALLED TO RECEIVE GOD'S WORD

Words matter. That is especially true when they proceed from the mouth of God. His words are more than words because they are generative and life-giving. He said, "Let there be light" (Genesis 1:3), and there was light. By his word, something as fundamental as light came into being. In the New Testament, we learn that all scripture is "God-breathed" (II Timothy 3:16). The Apostle Peter tells us that the authors of the Bible were not simply giving their opinions but were writing as "carried along by the Spirit" (II Peter 1:21). God's words are powerful, trustworthy (Psalm 33:4), and authoritative (II Timothy 3:16-17).

Putting these ideas together, we arrive at the doctrinal position that the Bible is our "only rule of faith and practice." As we contemplate the importance of this concept to our faith, we must also consider the object of our faith, Jesus Christ. The Gospel of John describes him as the *Logos*, or the Word. The generative, life-giving power of the Word of God is embodied in the person of Jesus, bringing rich meaning to the claims of Colossians 1:16 that he is the one through whom all things were made and who sustains all things. It is impossible to separate Jesus from the eternal Word of God because he *is* the Word. He is the fulfillment of the Old Testament promises. He is the central character of the Gospels. He is the object of Faith described in the New Testament epistles. He is the Worthy Lamb of Revelation, who rules and reigns in heaven. In summary, the Bible is more than a book of human wisdom or religious writings. It is the source of truth and light and is the very Word of God.

If all of this is true, if the Bible truly is the eternal Word of God as it claims to be, how should we respond to it? The Westminster Confession section 1:4 gives a very good answer, "The authority of the Holy Scripture, for which it ought to be believed, and obeyed, dependeth not upon the testimony of any man or church; but wholly upon God (who is truth itself) the author thereof: and therefore it is to be received because it is the Word of God."[1] We are called to receive God's Word. Why? Because "All Scripture is breathed out by God and profitable for teaching, for reproof, for correction, and for training in righteousness, that the man of God may be complete, equipped for every good work" (II Timothy 3:16-17). Despite our tendency to doubt God's Word at times and our tendency to adopt the world's views about it, scripture is a gift from a patient God, reminding us that he is faithful

---

1. G.I. Williamson, *The Westminster Confession of Faith for Study Classes* (Philadelphia: Presbyterian and Reformed Publishing Company, 1964), 4.

and not far away. In it, we learn that he knows us and desires us to flourish.

To receive scripture means to accept it, submit to it, study it, and share it with others. John Calvin writes, "Our wisdom ought to be nothing else than to embrace with humble teachableness, and at least without finding fault, whatever is taught in Sacred Scripture."[2] Without God's Word, we can know very little of our own anthropology. We can know nothing of the metanarrative that grounds us: Creation, Fall, Redemption, and Consummation. We can know nothing of Jesus, our Lord and Savior who died that we might live. We can know of God's existence simply by looking at his Creation (Romans 1:20), but it is only through scripture that we can understand God's plan of salvation and his design and desires for human life. Receiving God's Word means embracing its story, its vision, and its precepts. It means building our lives around it. In Psalm 19:7, we read that "The Law of the Lord is perfect, reviving the soul." This means that God's way for us, that is, his design for us, is perfect and perfectly explained in the pages of his Word.

There are many in the world who read the Bible yet do not believe a word of it. Others read it and receive it in faith. How can we explain this difference? First, we must understand that the Bible is not a magic decoder ring or talisman such that anyone who reads it will suddenly be

---

2. John Calvin, *Institutes of the Christian Religion*, J.T. McNeill, ed. and F.L. Battles, trans. (Philadelphia: The Westminster Press, 1960), 237.

spiritually enlightened. It is only by the Holy Spirit that anyone can come to believe the Word of God. Jesus told the disciples that the Holy Spirit would come to teach us all things and remind us of all Jesus had said (John 14:26). He went on to say that the Holy Spirit will guide us in all truth and prepare us for what is to come (John 16:23). Faith to believe the Bible is a gift of God (Ephesians 2:8-9). These truths are a comfort because in them, we know that the Holy Spirit is working toward the transformation of our minds and hearts, that is he is working toward our sanctification. It is also a comfort knowing that as we go out to share the truths of God's Word, it is ultimately the Holy Spirit that does the work of convicting others. These truths, while difficult to understand in one sense, can be a great comfort and motivator for sharing the gospel.

As followers of Christ, we are called to receive his Word. This can be difficult at times because we have doubts or worldly ideas that lead to confusion. In Romans 12:2, the Apostle Paul commands us to no longer conform to the pattern of the world but to transform our minds. He is speaking about moving away from worldly values and ideas and instead aligning ourselves with God's Word. As we noted in the last chapter, Paul is saying that we are already conformed to the pattern of the world and that there is now work to do to reform ourselves in the power of the Holy Spirit. Referring to the world, Paul is talking about the cultural values, norms, practices, and systems of thought that are opposed to the truth of scripture. On one extreme, this could mean *atheism* that not only denies that the Bible is the Word of God but also denies there is any God at all. In an atheistic worldview, the Bible is nothing more than a set of human myths and stories, certainly not something to base one's life upon. At the other extreme is the individual who claims to worship God but who has embraced ideologies that cast doubt on the Bible as anything more than human writing. At this end of the spectrum, people — often academics, but even some church leaders — have come to believe that Jesus is more of a metaphor rather than a real man, that many of the social commands were only applicable in the culture of the day, or that many of the books of the Bible were not actually written under the inspiration of the Holy Spirit. The Bible addresses and summarizes these issues in Paul's first letter to the Corinthians, which says that the message of the Cross is foolishness to the world (I Corinthians 1:18). As followers of Christ, once we have received his Word, we let it change us. As we step into a doubting and skeptical world, it is important to remember that we are called to go out as winsome, patient, and loving representatives of Christ. We are called to go humbly, extending grace to others, even those who deny the authority and validity of the Bible.

How can we grow in our knowledge of scripture and the wisdom it contains? There are many ways to grow in godly knowledge and wisdom. In fact, you will benefit from trying various things throughout your life. Here are three suggestions to get you started:

1. *Develop the habits of personal Bible reading.* If the regular reading of scripture is not your current habit, we encourage you to work on this during your Fellows

year. Some find it better to read in the morning, others at night. Some prefer to read long passages, while others prefer verse-by-verse study. Some prefer to read silently, others aloud. Some like to read along while listening to an audio Bible. Still others prefer to mix it up, using differing methods in various seasons of life. All of these are great ways to get into the habit of personal Bible reading. Try them all until you settle on the ones that work for you.

2. *Talk about scripture.* In addition to reading the Bible, talking about it with others is also a helpful discipline. A church small group, Bible study, or an informal friend gathering can be a great way to become conversant with God's Word. Speaking about it will help you recall and apply scripture to your life. It will also help you teach, disciple, and encourage others.

3. *Explore memorization.* Being able to recall passages of scripture is a powerful tool. It not only helps with personal growth but will also be an encouragement to others. Remember that in most of history, God's people did not have personal copies of the Bible at home. They mainly heard it read aloud in synagogues or churches. Memorization was the only option. You can do it!

## SCRIPTURE READINGS

And God said, "Let there be light," and there was light. And God saw that the light was good. And God separated the light from the darkness. – Genesis 1:3-4

So shall my word be that goes out from my mouth; it shall not return to me empty, but it shall accomplish that which I purpose, and shall succeed in the thing for which I sent it. Isaiah – 55:11

The law of the Lord is perfect, reviving the soul; the testimony of the Lord is sure, making wise the simple; – Psalm 19:7

Your word is a lamp to my feet and a light to my path. – Psalm 119:105

Heaven and earth will pass away, but my words will not pass away. – Matthew 24:35

In the beginning was the Word, and the Word was with God, and the Word was God. He was in the beginning with God. All things were made through him, and without him was not anything made that was made. In him was life, and the life was the light of men. The light shines in the darkness, and the darkness has not overcome it. – John 1:1-5

But the Helper, the Holy Spirit, whom the Father will send in my name, he will teach you all things and bring to your remembrance all that I have said to you. – John 14:26

So faith comes from hearing, and hearing through the word of Christ. – Romans 10:17

For whatever was written in former days was written for our instruction, that through endurance and through the encouragement of the Scriptures we might have hope. – Romans 15:4

For the word of the cross is folly to those who are perishing, but to us who are being saved it is the power of God. – I Corinthians 1:18

All Scripture is God-breathed and is useful for teaching, rebuking, correcting, and training in righteousness, so that the servant of God may be thoroughly equipped for every good work. – II Timothy 3:16-17 (NIV)

For no prophecy was ever produced by the will of man, but men spoke from God as they were carried along by the Holy Spirit. – II Peter 1:21

## DISCUSSION QUESTIONS

1. In this chapter, it is proposed that we "receive" God's Word. That is, we are called to read, digest, absorb, and be changed by it. Has this been your approach to the Bible? In what ways do you find it difficult to embrace and apply the words of scripture to your whole life?

2. In John 1, Jesus is described as the "Word" that was with God in the beginning and *is* God. What does this

mean to you? How does this message from John impact the way you see and understand Jesus as the Word of God?

3. Through the centuries, people have found many aspects of the Bible difficult to believe and accept. What are those for you? How do you deal with these passages? Do you ignore them? Do you try to explain them away? Do you ask God to give you special insight beyond scripture that would make them more acceptable to you or to others?

4. Regular reading and meditation on God's Word are good spiritual practices. Talk with your group about your own practices of reading and meditation on scripture. What has gone well? What is a struggle? How can friends help you grow in this area of your life?

5. What was the role of scripture in your home growing up? Was it read aloud? Was it ignored? Was there skepticism about it? How has this impacted your own views of the Bible? How do you want to maintain or change these practices in your life, especially when you think about possibly having your own family some day?

6. Consider the definition of *receive* found in this chapter (i.e., to receive scripture means to know it, accept it, submit to it, and share it with others). If you could change one thing about how Christians receive and interact with God's Word, what would it be?

# 5

# CALLED TO WORK AND CONTRIBUTE TO FLOURISHING

The very first words of scripture tell us, "In the beginning, God *created* the heavens and the earth" (Genesis 1:1). God is the Creator God, the one who makes. As we have already discussed in Chapter 1, God is not an impersonal, distant God. He is knowable and actively involved in our lives. Colossians 1 and Hebrews 1 celebrate the idea that Jesus, the second person of the Trinity, is the one through whom all things were made and the one who holds all things together. And we are made to be like him (Genesis 1:27). Paul charges us to be "imitators of God" (Ephesians 5:1). Unlike any other part of Creation, human beings are image-bearers made to reflect God's character, including the fact that he is a worker.

In so many ways, scripture celebrates God's work and creativity. Amos 4:13 is a great example. It says, "For behold, he who forms the mountains and creates the wind, and declares to man what is his thought, who makes the morning darkness, and treads on the heights of the earth

— the Lord, the God of hosts, is his name!" As image-bearers, part of our being, identity, and purpose are found in creative work. We honor God by working and applying the creative ability he has given us. We honor him when we help others by making useful things or providing great services. Work is good because it is one of the ways we celebrate God's character-reflecting design for humanity.

It is worth taking time to reflect on the relationship between God, us, and work. At times, it can seem that God is distant or only interested in the "spiritual" aspects of our lives. Some of the tasks associated with our work — bookkeeping, repairing a broken tool, cleaning a table in a restaurant — can seem irrelevant or insignificant compared with preaching the gospel, reaching the lost, or healing the sick. In her research, author and writer Amy Sherman found that many Christians "have limited vision for what it means to partner with God at work, to bring meaning to their work or to accomplish kingdom purposes in and through their work."[1] In Colossians 3:23, Paul calls us not to think this way. He challenges us to do *all we do* as unto the Lord. Every task we do is important to God, from sorting the laundry to launching a new business. He invites us to transform our thoughts about work to see that he is the One in whom we live, move, and have our being (Acts 17:28), regardless of what we are doing at that moment. It is not God who is distant from us; but us from him.

---

1. Amy Sherman, *Kingdom Calling: Vocational Stewardship for the Common Good* (Downer's Grove: Intervarsity Press, 2011), 100.

We have come to believe that there are parts of our lives about which God cares a lot, and other parts for which he cares less. This is a false dichotomy. That God is present with us in every little thing we do is a powerful idea and a daily encouragement as we head into work. There is freedom and comfort in knowing that God cares about even the smallest, most ordinary tasks of our day. The Cultural Mandate (Genesis 1:26-28) is alive and well, and God is inviting us to join him in his work, no matter what we are doing. Rather than seeing work as drudgery and something that pulls us away from what we want to be doing, we can see work as an opportunity to be close to God in what *he* is doing. A vision of work transformed by the gospel, despite our daily challenges and frustrations, is an opportunity to see that our work is a means by which we live in the presence of God, guided by him, working alongside him.

If work is so great, why does it cause so much stress in our lives? Why is workplace turnover so high? Why do so many people dream about checking out of work and retiring early? The answer is that, like everything else in Creation, work was impacted by the Fall. Genesis 3:17-19 tells us that work was made harder after the Fall. Creation now pushes against us with "thorns and thistles." Work has also become more difficult because of relational corruption. Our selfish attitudes, our misunderstanding of God's good design, our lack of commitment — all of these are the result of our sin. We expect work to satisfy our souls even though soul-satisfaction is something only Jesus can do. Rather than seeing work as a way to serve and bring flourishing into the world, we often focus on what work can do *for us* — make us comfortably wealthy, give us a sense of power and control, bestow status, make a name for us in our field. Or sometimes, we focus on our perception of what work is doing *to us* — keeping us from having fun or pressing in on our sensibilities about authority and significance.

In addition to our own sinful tendencies about work, the world gives and reinforces many unhelpful messages about work as well. As an example, consider recent movies you have seen. How are wealthy investors, executives, artists, musicians, and blue-collar workers portrayed? People in these roles are often portrayed, through consistent archetypal tropes, in ways that reflect the idea that work is bad and that freeing yourself from work is good. "Just follow your heart and you'll be happy" is often the message. Contrary to many of the world's ideas about work, we are not only called to work because God is a worker, but we are called to be part of bringing value and redemption through our work.

On the surface, the world's ideas about work are attractive and seemingly wise. Perhaps you have heard people say, "if you find the job you love, you'll never work a day in your life." This common saying is worthy of some reflection. In it is the implication that work, or at least the sense that work feels like work, is undesirable. It implies that we should try to find work that does not feel like work, that is not hard, or that requires little or no effort. Perhaps you have heard of concepts like the "4-hour work week,"[2] which suggests that by just working cleverly enough, we can mostly avoid work. Again, the implication is that work is a necessary evil or burden and creating more play or leisure time is the goal. These ideas do not prove true in practice and are not sustainable, and yet they seem so enticing (and they sell a lot of books!). Why? Because we have come to believe that work is not truly good. The mindset behind these ideas is that tedious work, hard tasks, and being under the authority of another are to be avoided.

Under the influence of these ideas, many have developed significant fears about work. Common fears held by young adults include "getting stuck," "being lonely in my cubicle," and "doing boring or insignificant tasks." Since cubicles, individualized work, and routine tasks are common for virtually all entry-level professional positions, it is easy to see that worldly wisdom has set up nearly all young people for disappointment right from the start.

Confusingly, the world also offers inconsistent and conflicting messages about work and compensation. For example, the life of leisure is often idealized in pop culture, film, and literature. However, the acquisition of the wealth required to live such a life is often depicted as motivated only by greed. Consider the impoverished and misunderstood artist or musician depicted in film. They

---

2. Timothy Ferriss. *The 4-Hour Workweek: Escape 9-5, Live Anywhere, and Join the New Rich* (New York: Crown Publishing, 2007).

are often shown to be overcoming the odds to find their voice or unique sound. This sort of coming-of-age story is celebrated, while the later-in-life, successful artist or musician is often depicted as lost or even corrupted by the morass of record sales and attention-seeking. Are these films and books teaching us something about work or are they merely reinforcing the ideas and biases we already have? Either way, our challenge is to follow the Apostle Paul's call to no longer conform to the pattern of the world, but to be renewed by the transforming of our minds (Romans 12:2).

What if we could have a very different approach and attitude toward work? What if we moved beyond the archetypal tropes and messages presented to us by the culture of the world? What if, instead, we adopted a biblical perspective of work, one that understands that work is good but broken because of the Fall. What if we could stop expecting work to satisfy our souls and fulfill our longings, but instead pursued work as a way to worship God by using our gifts and abilities and to serve and bless colleagues, supervisors, and clients? To achieve such a transformation of heart and mind, we truly would need to turn from the pattern of the world's thinking about work, careers, and success. We would need to have a much bigger view of work, embracing its Creational design and Redemptive motivations.

In his book, *You Are What You Love*, Dr. James K. A. Smith suggests that we are made to worship and that we are worshipping all the time, albeit not always the God of the Bible.[3] We are made to love God with our whole being — heart, soul, and strength. And, as we studied in Chapter 2, we are called to love our neighbors as ourselves (Leviticus 19:18; Mark 12:31). When are these commands to love God and love others to be applied? Always! When we go to work, we are called to love God and neighbor. And yet, as discussed earlier, we so often go to work focused on ourselves, on our own anxieties, our need to be satisfied, etc. God is calling us away from the world's pattern of thought and into his pattern of thought. He is calling us away from selfishness at work and into others-oriented love at work. He is calling us to be like him even when we go to work. Wrestling with these issues is not easy. Confronting idols and cultural norms involves difficult soul-searching. And yet, God is inviting you into it. By the power of the Holy Spirit, you can do this!

To close this chapter, consider another aspect of God's design for work. When someone performs a service for you, cutting your hair for example, you pay them. Why? Because they have done something of value for you and the money paid is a representation of that value. Workers create value. Creating value, whether we accept payment for it or not, is part of what it means to work. In other words, work has economic implications. When we integrate the idea that God made us to work with the idea that work creates value, we must also consider that God

---

3. James K.A. Smith, *You Are What You Love: The Spiritual Power of Habit* (Grand Rapids: Brazos Press, 2016).

has created an economic system as part of the fabric of Creation.⁴ We call this economic system *stewardship*. Remember that Adam was placed in the Garden to work it and to keep it (Genesis 2:15). That is, he was placed there as a steward. We, too, are here to work and keep the world.

In his book *Visions of Vocation*, Dr. Steve Garber suggests that we are responsible for the world in which we live.⁵ Our work is not simply for our own material advancement and personal gain. In reflecting upon our role to create value for others through our work, economist Anne Rathbone Bradley writes, "You have something to offer the world, and through your gifts and talents you can create something better than what you were born into. You have an eternal legacy to leave. These gifts and talents position you to contribute to the flourishing of the world. Whether you use your gifts to go into law, construction, or music, you can create something that can glorify God and improve other people's lives."⁶

As we go to work, it is imperative that we consider the resources we consume and the value we create. Our time, other peoples' time, raw materials, money — these are all limited resources that we are called to use to the

---

4. Tom Nelson, *The Economics of Neighborly Love: Investing in Your Community's Compassion and Capacity* (Downer's Grove: Intervarsity Press, 2017).

5. Steven Garber, *Visions of Vocation: Common Grace for the Common Good* (Downer's Grove: Intervarsity Press, 2014).

6. Anne Rathbone Bradley, *How to be Content but not Complacent* (The Gospel Coalition, June 25, 2014).

glory of God and for the advancement of the common good.[7] Limited resources can be wasted if we are not careful or if we are selfish. Part of our responsibility as God's image-bearers is to understand and care for the world and one another as stewards of this place. Comprehending this concept requires that we develop a deep understanding of the economic implications of work.

## SCRIPTURE READINGS

In the beginning, God created the heavens and the earth. – Genesis 1:1

And God blessed them. And God said to them, "Be fruitful and multiply and fill the earth and subdue it, and have dominion over the fish of the sea and over the birds of the heavens and over every living thing that moves on the earth." – Genesis 1:28

The Lord God took the man and put him in the garden of Eden to work it and keep it. – Genesis 2:15

And to Adam he said, "Because you have listened to the voice of your wife and have eaten of the tree of which I commanded you, 'You shall not eat of it,' cursed is the

---

7. Jake Meador. *In Search of the Common Good: Christian Fidelity in a Fractured World* (Downer's Grove: Intervarsity Press, 2019).

ground because of you; in pain you shall eat of it all the days of your life; thorns and thistles it shall bring forth for you; and you shall eat the plants of the field. By the sweat of your face you shall eat bread, till you return to the ground, for out of it you were taken; for you are dust, and to dust you shall return." – Genesis 3:17-19

Remember the Sabbath day, to keep it holy. Six days you shall labor, and do all your work, but the seventh day is a Sabbath to the Lord your God. – Exodus 20:8-10

You shall not oppress a hired worker who is poor and needy, whether he is one of your brothers or one of the sojourners who are in your land within your towns. – Deuteronomy 24:14

Let the favor of the Lord our God be upon us, and establish the work of our hands upon us; yes, establish the work of our hands! – Psalm 90:17

Go to the ant, O sluggard; consider her ways, and be wise. Without having any chief, officer, or ruler, she prepares her bread in summer and gathers her food in harvest. – Proverbs 6:6-8

Whoever works his land will have plenty of bread, but he who follows worthless pursuits lacks sense. – Proverbs 12:11

In all toil there is profit, but mere talk tends only to poverty. – Proverbs 14:23

Commit your work to the Lord, and your plans will be established. – Proverbs 16:3

Thus says the Lord of hosts, the God of Israel, to all the exiles whom I have sent into exile from Jerusalem to Babylon: Build houses and live in them; plant gardens and eat their produce. Take wives and have sons and daughters; take wives for your sons, and give your daughters in marriage, that they may bear sons and daughters; multiply there, and do not decrease. But seek the welfare of the city where I have sent you into exile, and pray to the Lord on its behalf, for in its welfare you will find your welfare. – Jeremiah 29:4-7

Let all that you do be done in love. – I Corinthians 16:14

And let us not grow weary of doing good, for in due season we will reap, if we do not give up. So then, as we have opportunity, let us do good to everyone, and especially to those who are of the household of faith. – Galatians 6:9-10

Let the thief no longer steal, but rather let him labor, doing honest work with his own hands, so that he may have something to share with anyone in need. –Ephesians 4:28

Bondservants, obey in everything those who are your earthly masters, not by way of eye-service, as people-pleasers, but with sincerity of heart, fearing the Lord. Whatever you do, work heartily, as for the Lord and not for men, knowing that from the Lord you will receive the inheritance as your reward. You are serving the Lord Christ. – Colossians 3:22-24

But if anyone does not provide for his relatives, and especially for members of his household, he has denied the faith and is worse than an unbeliever. – I Timothy 5:8

For even when we were with you, we would give you this command: If anyone is not willing to work, let him not eat. For we hear that some among you walk in idleness, not busy at work, but busybodies. Now such persons we command and encourage in the Lord Jesus Christ to do their work quietly and to earn their own living. As for you, brothers, do not grow weary in doing good. – I Thessalonians 3:10-13

But we urge you, brothers, to do this more and more, and to aspire to live quietly, and to mind your own affairs, and to work with your hands, as we instructed you. – I Thessalonians 4:10-11

## DISCUSSION QUESTIONS

1. God works. He creates, sustains, and re-creates. He works, and work is good. How does this aspect of God's character sit with you? How can we keep this aspect of his character in the front of our minds as we worship him in all areas of life?

2. As image-bearers, we are workers. How does this truth sit with you and impact the way you think about yourself? How does the idea that we are made to co-create with God impact your understanding of your

relationship with him? How does this impact your thoughts about work?

3. Do you trust God — really — with your career and vocational dreams? Do you believe God is truly working for your good in this aspect of your life? Explain.

4. In our sin, we have broken attitudes and motivations toward work. Some of us make work more than it is designed to be. Others seek to avoid work as much as possible. How have these patterns played out in your life?

5. As a Fellow, you recently started a new job. In what ways have you been you pleasantly surprised about the work you are doing? In what ways have you been disappointed by it? Do you find yourself comparing your job with jobs your friends have? How are you processing the idea that your job is exactly where God wants you to be right now?

6. The world tells us a lot of things about work. What are some of the world's ideas about work — especially those that are inconsistent with God's Word —that have impacted the way you think about and approach work?

7. The Proverbs calls us to be diligent people that approach our work with integrity and sincere effort. Is this a challenge for you? Explain.

8. When we work well, we create value. In exchange for the value we create, employers pay us. There is a wide range of ideas about economic value creation and reward distribution, ranging from socialist-collectivist ideas to capitalistic-objectivist ideas. Society is very divided over these ideas. What role can and should Christians play in this discussion?

# 6

# CALLED TO REST

There are countless books, websites, and how-to videos about working less, finding work-life balance, and trying to find inner peace and tranquility. Why so many? Because there is a market for these ideas! In our desperation to find rest, we have become willing to seek out and believe all sorts of ideas and theories about what we need. The irony for believers is that God tells us plainly what we need: Him. We need hearts and minds that are inclined toward him and willing to live the way he has designed us to live. Many popular ideas about rest sound good on the surface, but underneath reveal a misunderstanding of God's good design for work and rest. For example, have you ever dissected the phrase *work-life balance*? It casts a shadow on work as something that is not part of life but something opposed to life. This phrase suggests that work is something that must be held in balance or tension with life. Contrary to this phrase, we explored in the previous chapter that work is good and part of God's design for a good life. The challenge is not to try to find work-life balance but to find a biblically grounded work-rest balance.

God created all things in six days. On the seventh day, he rested from creating. This showed something of God's character. He stopped to enjoy the good things he had made. Having completed six days of work, he rested on the seventh day. In doing this, he set the pattern for us. That pattern is a season of work followed by a season of rest. He gave it to us in the fourth commandment, which tells us that we are to work six days and then rest one day (Exodus 20:8-11). This commandment is not just a rule to control us. It was given to us for our good (Mark 2:27). It is good for us to be imitators of God, that is, people who live according to his character. When our rest reflects God's good design for us, we flourish the most. When our rest does not reflect his good design, there is less flourishing.

Rest in the Bible comes in various shapes and sizes. In addition to the creational pattern of weekly rest, six days of work followed by one day of rest, we also see patterns of daily rest and nightly sleep (Psalm 4:8; Ecclesiastes 5:12). There is also a conceptual sort of rest that can only be found in genuine faith. In trusting that God loves us and is working out all things for our good, we can rest and be at peace (Psalm 37:7; Isaiah 40:28-31). And, perhaps the most intimate rest we can find is offered to us in Christ himself. He bids us come and rest in him (Matthew 11:28-30). He invites us to put our faith in him, which is a deep abiding trust that he is the source of rest for our weary souls in a wearying world.

Interestingly, rest does not always mean not working. Well understood, true rest comes not just from the cessation of work, but we can experience true rest *in* the work itself. Jesus invites us to take on his yoke (Matthew 11:29). The imagery of this passage is that Jesus is the worker of the field, and we are the ox. He is guiding us, and we are drawing the tilling blade through the soil. It is an image of labor. At first glance and with modern sensibilities about work, that does not sound very restful. But in Christ and with a clear image of his design for flourishing, we know that Jesus' words are true. That is, his yoke is easy, and his burden is light. In other words, rest is not only found in the cessation of work but also in working *with* Christ, toward his mission and ends. Here in this deeper sense, rest becomes peace, *shalom*. In his book *How Then Should We Work*, Hugh Whelchel describes shalom as everything working together as it was intended to be — no strife, no waste, no anxiety.[1] What a glorious thought, that even our work might give us peace and rest!

Like most everything in our lives, we break rest. In our sin and rebellion against God, we fail to pursue true rest and peace, not only in our own lives but in our relationships with others. As much as we are made to rest in Christ and to be at peace with God, we end up in anxious strife more than any of us would like. We break rest in at least two ways. The most common way is that we idolize it. Interestingly, we do not idolize true rest as designed by God. We idolize rest as it is offered and idealized by the world. It is often more about leisure and

---

1. Hugh Whelchel, *How Then Should We Work: Rediscovering the Biblical Doctrine of Work* (Bloomington: Westbow Press, 2012).

play than it is about true, restorative rest. It is often more about keeping up and maintaining an image than it is about true rest. What do we see in the best social media photos and videos? They usually feature people traveling, playing, or going out to eat. We are determined, it seems, to present an image of ourselves as fully embracing — and able to afford — a life of leisure, surrounded by friends, smiling, and laughing, hitting all the latest restaurants and bars, traveling to exotic places, wearing all the latest fashions. More than we would like to admit, our mental images and expectations of rest are formed mostly by worldly ideals and values. The pursuit of these ideals and values, when we dig deeply into them, is often exhausting and not restful at all. It is easy to fall into the trap that suggests rest equals play. And, in a cruel twist, the image of the leisurely life can contribute to our sense of burden and anxiety. Even in our leisure, we can strive to keep up with those around us or those we see on social media. Our need to belong to the right group, to be admired, to be fashionable, and our tendency to jealously compare ourselves to others are just some of the ways we fail to rest well.

The second way we commonly break rest is by failing to embrace work rightly. On one extreme, some of us are drawn to workaholism. The sense of achievement, accomplishment, or even simply the enjoyment of work draws us into a pattern of seven and zero, rather than six and one. Instead of devoting hours every day to friends and family, to meditation and reflection, we inch our way toward the 14-hour workday. For the workaholic, there is no rest. Even when we appear to be resting, our minds are hard at work.

For others, broken rest is not about workaholism but about other ways that we keep our minds on edge. We procrastinate. We expect perfection. We avoid conflict. We are afraid to fail. There is a long list of complex and intertwined behaviors that contribute to workplace anxiety. In his book, *Perfecting Ourselves to Death*, Dr. Richard Winter suggests that procrastinators are often perfectionists in disguise.[2] They cannot stand the idea of not being perfect, so they keep putting off work until they have created the excuse, "Oh, I just did not have enough time to do it properly." And, of course, some break God's design for rest simply by avoiding work and the responsibilities that go with it. In this mindset, work is seen as a necessary evil rather than a good thing from God. As a result, the avoidance of work is seen as the goal of a successful life. For some, it is not simply about the avoidance of work, but the avoidance of working for another person. When we dissect these desires, it is often the idols of pride, independence, and control making themselves known. Whether trapped by the world's ideas of rest or impaired by our own struggles with work and rest, the result is the same. We end up far from God's good design for us. Rather than seeking and finding godly rest, we settle for a facsimile that ultimately leaves us wanting.

---

2. Richard Winter. *Perfecting Ourselves to Death: The Pursuit of Excellence and the Perils of Perfectionism* (Downer's Grove: Intervarsity Press, 2005).

How can we get onto a path of healing in our work and rest? The discussion that accompanies this chapter will hopefully be the beginning of a journey to a better place for you. It is our desire that you and your Fellows community can have deep and fruitful conversation about this topic so that you can walk with and serve one another this year. There is a wonderful opportunity for you and your peers to grasp and embrace a biblical approach to work and rest that many in previous generations have struggled to find. To start the conversation, we propose a practice of rest rooted in scripture itself. We must transform our minds (Romans 12:2) and begin to think differently about rest so the physical and spiritual practice of rest can follow. Let us start with the inside and work toward the outside. We cannot continue to believe our broken approaches to rest will suddenly start to work, or that the world's "wisdom" about rest will suddenly become true. Instead, we need to look at the patterns of rest found in scripture and embrace them.

Scripture teaches weekly and daily habits of rest. It teaches that rest is not an escape from work, but an opportunity to reflect upon it. It teaches that only in Christ can we find true rest. Only as we take on his yoke (an image of work) can we truly find rest. Second, we must begin, even in simple ways, the patterns of daily and weekly rest. Rather than filling our daily rest time with comparative images that induce stress and anxiety, why not trade our social media time for a time of personal reflection or time with friends? Try daily Bible reading, meditation, and prayer. Spend a season of personal study on the verses that speak about work and rest, including those below. Do this in solitude each day and together each week. Finally, most Fellows programs set aside one day in seven as the Fellow's Sabbath. Discuss with your program leaders and other Fellows how you can truly embrace your Sabbath each week. This often means taking care of chores and to-do list items during the week, before and after work or class. Talking with other Christians about rest is helpful, especially when those discussions rest on scripture and point out ways that we are tempted to adopt worldly ideas and values about work and rest. The habits of daily and weekly rest will not form in one week. It will take time to build these practices into your life. Your Fellows year is designed to be a time for just such an endeavor.

## SCRIPTURE READINGS

And on the seventh day God finished his work that he had done, and he rested on the seventh day from all his work that he had done. So, God blessed the seventh day and made it holy, because on it God rested from all his work that he had done in Creation. – Genesis 2:2-3

Remember the Sabbath day, to keep it holy. Six days you shall labor, and do all your work, but the seventh day is a Sabbath to the Lord your God. On it you shall not do any work, you, or your son, or your daughter, your male servant, or your female servant, or your livestock, or the sojourner who is within your gates. For in six days the Lord made heaven and earth, the sea, and all that is in them, and rested on the seventh day. Therefore, the Lord blessed the Sabbath day and made it holy. – Exodus 20:8-11

In peace I will both lie down and sleep; for you alone, O Lord, make me dwell in safety. – Psalm 4:8

Be still before the Lord and wait patiently for him; fret not yourself over the one who prospers in his way, over the man who carries out evil devices! – Psalm 37:7

Sweet is the sleep of a laborer, whether he eats little or much, but the full stomach of the rich will not let him sleep. – Ecclesiastes 5:12

Have you not known? Have you not heard? The Lord is the everlasting God, the Creator of the ends of the earth. He does not faint or grow weary; his understanding is unsearchable. He gives power to the faint, and to him who has no might he increases strength. Even youths shall faint and be weary, and young men shall fall exhausted; but they who wait for the Lord shall renew their strength; they shall mount up with wings like eagles; they shall run and not be weary; they shall walk and not faint. Isaiah – 40:28-31

Come to me, all who labor and are heavy laden, and I will give you rest. Take my yoke upon you, and learn from me, for I am gentle and lowly in heart, and you will find rest for your souls. For my yoke is easy, and my burden is light. – Matthew 11:28-30

And he said to them, "The Sabbath was made for man, not man for the Sabbath. So, the Son of Man is lord even of the Sabbath." – Mark 2:27-28

Peace I leave with you; my peace I give to you. Not as the world gives do I give to you. Let not your hearts be troubled, neither let them be afraid. – John 14:27

I have said these things to you, that in me you may have peace. In the world you will have tribulation. But take heart; I have overcome the world. – John 16:33

Do not be anxious about anything, but in everything by prayer and supplication with thanksgiving let your requests be made known to God. And the peace of God, which surpasses all understanding, will guard your hearts and your minds in Christ Jesus. – Philippians 4:6-7

## DISCUSSION QUESTIONS

1. What were the patterns of work and rest that you observed in your childhood? How did your family's practices of these things impact you?

2. We are made to work. By working, we honor God's good design for us. We are also made to rest. In God's design of six and one, there is a perfect balance. And yet, we often want work to be more or less than six and rest to be less or more than one. What does this balance say about God? What do your preferences say about you?

3. Scripture offers both conceptual and practical insight about rest. Practically, we learn that rest is a life pattern — daily and weekly. Conceptually, we learn that Jesus is our rest. What do you find most intriguing about these ideas for your own life?

4. Have you been able to trust God by following his good pattern of rest? Or have you been determined to follow your own pattern or the wisdom of the world? Explain.

5. We break rest in many ways. For example, we cannot stop comparing ourselves to our friends. Rather than imagining a lifetime of the good work-rest pattern, we might imagine quitting altogether through early retirement, etc. Rather than embracing the hope we have in Christ, we might have become cynical about work and rest, resolving to just do what everyone else is doing. Describe the ways that you break rest.

6. Jesus offers to be our rest. It is not that he gives us this gift and then leaves. He is the gift. Peace and rest are only found in an ongoing, growing relationship with him. When you think of your friends who do not know Jesus, how does this idea impact your sense of the Great Commission (to go and make disciples of all people)? Does it motivate you to know that the only way your friends can know true peace and rest is by having a relationship with Jesus?

7. As a Fellows group, plan for how you will walk with each other the remainder of this year into a lifetime of

good work and good rest, with daily and weekly patterns and habits.

# SECTION 2

# SERVICE

This section is an exploration of our call to serve one another. Service is an inherent part of who we are made to be; that is, we are made to serve by God's design. This is arguably one of the most elegant and beautiful aspects of God's design of the human being.

We are image-bearers of the God who serves us by creating and sustaining not only us but also everything we need for life and flourishing. Jesus came as a human being, in the form of a servant. He came to serve the poor and widows and we are made to be like him.

Even though we are made to serve one another, we easily drift away from this aspect of God's design by focusing on ourselves. In this section, we will explore several aspects of servanthood. Like the other sections in this book, the focus will be on the biblical basis for servanthood as an essential element of the Christian life while also providing ideas for discussion. Remember, each chapter is meant to be a conversation starter. Run with each topic as you explore God's design for you.

# 7

# CALLED TO SERVE

When you imagine great servants, who comes to mind? Maybe you think about Mother Theresa, Nelson Mandela, or other famous people who have served on a grand scale. Maybe you think about family or friends who love to host people in their homes. But the greatest, most servant-hearted person in history is Jesus Christ. He left the riches of heaven to come to us as a human (II Corinthians 8:9). Like any other human being, he was subject to every temptation and weakness, and yet, was without sin.

The Apostle Paul tells us that Jesus lowered himself by becoming a human being, taking the very form of a servant (Philippians 2:7). In reading this passage, we learn that we, as humans, are servants. It is who we are. Also in this passage, we learn that Jesus is the King of servants, the perfect model, in whose footsteps we are to walk. Jesus tells us that he came not to be served but to serve (Matthew 20:28), and this is coming from the King of Kings and Lord of Lords! How much more, then, should we understand our own place, and our own calling in terms of servanthood? Jesus did not just do an act of service here and there. No, servanthood is integral to who he is. He came in the form of a servant. We are also in the form of servants. It is part of God's good design for us.

If it is true that to be human is to be a servant, then we ought to explore and understand what it means to serve. We need to be students of servanthood. Where should we start? Scripture explains that at the heart of servanthood is humility (Philippians 2:3-8). The Apostle Paul calls us to think of others more highly than ourselves and to put the interests of others before our own interests. In the definition of love in I Corinthians 13, we learn that love does not demand its own way. Why? Because to do so puts our way before the needs of others. It is easy to think that being a servant means one-time or one-off efforts, like serving in a soup kitchen on Thanksgiving morning. While there is nothing wrong with serving once a year in a soup kitchen, it is not the robust image of servanthood in the Bible. Servanthood is exemplified best in deep, sustained relationships. We might say that servanthood is a lifestyle for the Christian. It is a lifestyle marked by a focus on the interests of others rather than our own interests. It is a lifestyle that is willing to exchange worldly comforts for discomfort when required. It is a lifestyle in which serving is a sustained commitment more than a one-off effort.

Where should we serve? There is no shortage of needs in this world. Consider the global situation. Although the World Bank reports that abject poverty is declining globally,[1] World Vision reported that 193 million people in 53 countries were still experiencing acute food insecurity in 2021.[2] According to UNESCO, more than 118.5 million age-eligible girls around the world were not enrolled in primary education.[3] According to one researcher, over 1 billion people have died in the last 40 years without ever hearing the name of Jesus.[4] What about closer to home? According to a 2019 report by the U.S. Census Bureau, more than 11.6 percent of Americans in the largest U.S. cities were living below the poverty line.[5] According to the U.S. Department of Education, roughly 54 percent of American adults were unable to read above a sixth-grade level in 2020.[6] Alongside material needs, we must also consider the spiritual needs of people, specifically their need to know and trust Jesus for eternal life. The percentage of Americans that have an active faith in Christ has been dropping as a percentage of the population. Barna reported that the number of Americans that

---

1. The World Bank. *Decline of Global Extreme Poverty Continues but Has Slowed.* Press Release on September 19, 2018.

2. World Vision. *10 World Hunger Facts You Need to Know.* July 6, 2022.

3. UNESCO. *Her Atlas: Monitoring the Right to Education for Girls and Women.* January 2023.

4. Global Commission Partners. *The World and Christianity.* January 2023.

5. U.S. Census Bureau. *Poverty in the United States: 2021.* September 2022.

6. Barbara Bush Foundation for Family Literacy and Gallup, Inc. *Assessing the Economic Gains of Eradicating Illiteracy Nationally and Regionally in the United States.* September 8, 2020.

consider themselves to be Practicing Christians, a designation of active involvement in a local Bible-believing church, personal Bible study, etc., has declined to roughly 25 percent of American adults.[7] And what about even closer to home: the people in your life? Nearly all of us have friends, colleagues, and acquaintances that are suffering from loneliness, doubt, or discouragement. Maybe you know a single parent who struggles to find childcare or someone who is unable to take care of their home. What can we say to all of this? There is clearly no shortage of service opportunities for the people of God, whether on a global or national scale, or even just among our friends. There are opportunities to serve individually, in small groups, or as an entire church. If you are not already involved with an area of service, this Fellows year is the perfect time for you to explore God's call to serve.

Serving is Christlike and it contributes to the flourishing of the world. We can also find deep joy in serving. So, what keeps us from living lives of servanthood? Here are some examples:

1. *Avoiding the discomfort of service.* We must acknowledge that serving can be difficult and draining at times. It pushes against our personal time and sense of comfort.

---

7. Barna Group, LLC. *Signs of Decline & Hope Among Key Metrics of Faith.* March 4, 2020.

Sacrificial servanthood sometimes means dealing with people we find hard to love.

2. *Following the teaching of the world about boundaries and self-care.* While boundaries and self-care are not bad things in themselves, the wisdom of the world often involves these taking priority over the urgent needs of those around us. It is implied that we should only serve up to the point that we become hurt or uncomfortable in the process. Sometimes in the world's system of boundaries, there is little room for truly sacrificial service. While we need to be mindful of boundaries and self-care, we also must heed the call to be living sacrifices that are willing to go into hard places with hard people, even if that means some suffering on our part.

3. *Having a checkbox mentality.* A third way that we keep ourselves from Christlike service is that we give ourselves a pass through "checkbox" thinking. For example, maybe our only service is at the soup kitchen once a year, or by holding the door for an elderly person. While these are certainly kind actions, they can trick us into thinking that we did our good deed for the day and can now return to our normal, self-interested lives. The point is that we are called to *be* servants rather than to do acts of service from time to time.

4. *An unhelpful inner narrative.* For example, we might have a deep fear of failure or a sense that we do not know what we are doing. Or we may be unwilling to take on

menial tasks because, deep down, we think we are above such things. Perhaps we have convinced ourselves that service is someone else's job. Each of us has an inner narrative that, if not kept in check, keeps us from developing ourselves as servants.

5. *Convincing ourselves that the problems are just too big.* Cynicism might prevent us from getting involved. While it is often true that we need to start small in our service, we must remember that nothing is impossible with God (Luke 1:37). We need to wake up from our cynical inaction.

As each of us grows in servanthood, it is helpful to have a strategy or game plan. Here we suggest a very basic, easy-to-remember, 5-step approach to serving others. The first step is simply to start seeing the needs. We do not need to start by thinking about global problems. We can look at the needs of our own family, neighbors, and friend groups.

The second step is to do something. In our fear, lack of empathy, or aloofness, we often fail to start. Perhaps in our desire to be a hero or in control, we are reluctant to take a small role. Or perhaps we take something of an academic approach by just thinking and talking about the problems around us, without getting personally involved. Whatever the reason, we need to move beyond inaction to service. As James notes in his epistle, it does little good to walk past people with needs and to offer them no help (James 2:15-16).

The third step is to grow in your experience. This takes time. Passion is often our initial motivation for getting involved in a service area, but passion alone does not provide the knowledge and experience needed to address the challenging problems we face in the world. The knowledge and experience that will make you a credible servant leader will come from a combination of passion, experience, and relationships.

The fourth step is to lead others. Once you have developed knowledge and experience in the field, you will be able to credibly invite others into the work. Experience is the platform from which we can teach and train other servants. Section four of this book will give a lot more details about how we can lead in godly ways.

Finally, the fifth step is wisdom. Many attempts at service have gone wrong because we have not considered all the factors that contribute to the problem or have not established the kinds of relationships that are required to be part of a lasting solution. Sometimes, the very people that we intend to help end up getting hurt. In their book, *When Helping Hurts*, Steve Corbett and Brian Fikkert suggest, "If we reduce human beings to being simply physical — as Western thought is prone to do — our poverty-alleviation efforts will tend to focus on material solutions. But if we remember that humans are spiritual, social, psychological, and physical beings, our poverty-alleviation efforts will be more holistic in their design and execution."⁸ Serving in areas with long-term, systemic problems requires wisdom, planning, and most of all real relationships. It is essential that we understand that physical needs are just part of the problem.

Despite the Fall of Humanity and the emergence of sin, God is still on his original mission of building a God-honoring society. He is undoing the damage of the Fall by renewing all things (Revelation 21:5). One of the most exciting things about the Christian life is that rather than banishing us to eternal destruction, God is inviting us to be part of his work! He is calling us not to make names for ourselves or to be great in our own eyes, but to humble ourselves as servants, as he did when he became human in the person of Jesus Christ. What a glorious invitation! In her book, *In His Image*, author Jen Wilkin connects our servanthood to our image-bearing, specifically that we are called to reflect the mercy of God. She writes, "Mercy means relieving suffering, both physical and spiritual. In view of God's mercy, we sacrifice our own bodily comfort that others might find relief in their lack. We do this for those we love, certainly. But we also do this for those to whom we bear no obligation."⁹ Our challenge is this:

---

8. Steve Corbett and Brian Fikkert, *When Helping Hurts: How to Alleviate Poverty without Hurting the Poor...and Yourself* (Chicago: Moody Publishers, 2014), 60.

9. Jen Wilkin, In His Image: *10 Ways God Calls Us to Reflect His Character* (Wheaton: Crossway, 2018) ,79.

Open our eyes and get to work, to move beyond talk, and get our hands dirty engaging with those in need around us.

## SCRIPTURE READINGS

For there will never cease to be poor in the land. Therefore, I command you, "You shall open your hand to your brother, to the needy and the poor in your land." – Deuteronomy 15:1

Whoever despises his neighbor is a sinner, but blessed is he who is generous to the poor. – Proverbs 14:21

If you pour yourself out for the hungry and satisfy the desire of the afflicted, then shall your light rise in the darkness and your gloom be as the noonday. – Isaiah 58:10

Even as the Son of Man came not to be served but to serve, and to give his life as a ransom for many. – Matthew 20:28

The greatest among you shall be your servant. – Matthew 23:11

When he had washed their feet and put on his outer garments and resumed his place, he said to them, "Do you understand what I have done to you? You call me Teacher and Lord, and you are right, for so I am. If I then, your Lord and Teacher, have washed your feet, you also ought to wash one another's feet." – John 13:12-14

For you were called to freedom, brothers. Only do not use your freedom as an opportunity for the flesh, but through love serve one another. – Galatians 5:13

Do nothing from selfish ambition or conceit, but in humility count others more significant than yourselves. Let each of you look not only to his own interests, but also to the interests of others. Have this mind among yourselves, which is yours in Christ Jesus, who, though he was in the form of God, did not count equality with God a thing to be grasped, but emptied himself, by taking the form of a servant, being born in the likeness of men. And being found in human form, he humbled himself by becoming obedient to the point of death, even death on a cross. – Philippians 2:3-8

As each has received a gift, use it to serve one another, as good stewards of God's varied grace. – I Peter 4:10

If a brother or sister is poorly clothed and lacking in daily food, and one of you says to them, "Go in peace, be warmed and filled," without giving them the things needed for the body, what good is that? – James 2:15-16

## DISCUSSION QUESTIONS

1. Who are the people in your life that serve as living examples of sustained servanthood? Describe one of them.

2. What are some ways people have served you well, personally? What makes these examples stand out for you? What makes them special?

3. After washing the disciples' feet, Jesus instructed them to go and do likewise. He tells us that by our love for one another, the world will know we are his disciples. As you receive these commands to love through servanthood, what is your response? Are you excited to "Go!"? Are you apprehensive?

4. The Apostle Paul tells us that Jesus came "in the very form of a servant." What does this mean to you?

5. What are some of the ways God has uniquely gifted you to serve others? Give some examples of how you have served using these gifts in the past.

6. Have you experienced significant failures in your attempts to serve? Have you tried to help and ended up hurting people? What did this mean for them? ...and for you?

7. Sometimes we are called to serve and lead in areas where we have little or no experience. What are some ways we can prepare ourselves for the various types of service we will be called to provide? How do you feel about serving and leading others in areas where you lack experience and have no role models?

# 8

# JUSTICE AND MERCY: FIRST PRINCIPLES OF SERVICE

For all the beauty we see in God's Creation, we must admit that the world can also be a difficult place. Our poor treatment of one another started quickly after the Fall. Cain, the first child born into this world, murdered his brother, the second child born into this world. From our earliest days, human society has been stained by all sorts of evil — murder, deception, theft, enslavement, greed, hatred, and promiscuity. Our sins are an abomination to God because they are an affront to his character (Isaiah 59:2). They are out of alignment with his good design for us. And they are unjust acts that we commit against God and one another.

These unjust acts are not always committed at the individual level. History is filled with unjust acts committed against entire groups of people: the transatlantic slave trade, the Holocaust of World War II, the Killing Fields of Cambodia. The ripple effects and societal remnants of these and other atrocities have been felt for generations.

Meditating on this history of human injustice should leave us mournful and full of lament. And yet, despite these atrocities, there is hope in Christ. And in that hope, there is work for us to do. God calls us to be people of justice and mercy (Micah 6:8). He is not calling us simply to think about these things but to be doers of them. He is calling us to be ambassadors of reconciliation and redemption. He is calling us not to wallow in the ugliness of a broken world or to stick our heads in the sand but to be part of his restorative work. Pursuing these callings requires us to understand that the biblical prescription for justice and mercy will be different from the world's prescription. As we have already discussed, the world's view of truth and reality is generally misaligned with God's view. So, as we set out on our path to learn about justice and mercy, we should be clear about what God requires of us.

Micah 6:8 is a well-known passage on justice and mercy. The context of this text is a courtroom scene. God was giving an indictment against his people. He was angry about the way they treated each other and the way they engaged in illegitimate forms of worship. In the middle of the chapter, he poses the question: What does God require of you? He answers his own question: to do justice, love mercy, and walk humbly with God. He is not presenting justice and mercy as two opposing ideas between which we must find a delicate balance. We often understand justice as getting what you deserve (e.g., punishment for wrongdoing) and mercy as getting something you do not deserve (e.g., not getting punished for wrong-doing). Interestingly, in the Hebrew language, this text can be read not as two separate concepts but as a single, intertwined concept, something like "justice-mercy."[1] God is the God of justice, full stop. And he is the God of mercy, full stop. Within God, we know there is no contradiction (II Timothy 2:13; Titus 1:2). He is perfect and whole. In God, justice and mercy are complete and perfect. They are not opposing ideas precariously balanced within him. Even though we tend to separate these ideas, God is challenging us to understand them as he does: united in him.

It is a worthy reflection to consider the concepts of justice and mercy in your own life and relationship with Christ. Our sin has separated us from God as a matter of justice. And yet, in his mercy, Jesus has taken the punishment upon himself (i.e., justice) that should have come to us (i.e., mercy). The justice that was due to us was laid upon him. And having completed the work of salvation on the Cross, he offers his mercy to us — full forgiveness and adoption. Theologians refer to this concept as "double imputation." Our sin was imputed to Christ and his righteousness was imputed to us (II Corinthians 5:21). When we understand salvation this way, we are well on our way to understanding the kind of justice-mercy we are to promote in the world today.

Scripture is clear about the call to justice and the call away from injustice. Christians are called away from the greed that would inspire some to enslave others for profit. We are called away from the envy and covetousness

---

1. Bruce Waltke, *A Commentary on Micah* (Grand Rapids: William B. Eerdmans Publishing Company, 2008).

that drive theft, corrupt business and government schemes, and other manipulations. We are called away from the hatred, disrespect, and disregard that are at the heart of racism and other forms of bigotry. We are called not only to keep ourselves from these sins but to call them out and work against them in society (Proverbs 31:8-9). We are called to love and care for the poor, infirm, widows, immigrants, and downtrodden, those whom scripture calls the "least of these" (Matthew 25:40). In the parable of the Good Samaritan (Luke 10:25-37), Jesus challenges us to cross cultural and societal boundaries to serve and care for one another. For example, in his missionary travels across Asia Minor and Europe, Paul encouraged the churches to give financial support to the suffering church in Jerusalem (1 Cor 16:1-4; 2 Cor 8:1-9:15; Rom 15:14-32).

The Apostle James teaches that seeing needs and doing nothing about them is both unjust and unmerciful (James 2:15-17). In his book *Generous Justice*, Tim Keller writes this reflection of Jesus' life in terms of justice and mercy, "Jesus, in his incarnation, 'moved in' with the poor. He lived with, ate with, and associated with the socially ostracized. He raised the son of the poor widow and showed the greatest respect to the immoral woman who was a social outcast. Indeed, Jesus spoke with women in public, something that a man with any standing in society would not have done, but Jesus resisted the sexism of his day."[2]

As we consider real-life justice and mercy situations, we need to check ourselves. When you think about the brokenness of the world today, are you more inclined toward justice or mercy? Are you ready to adopt and pursue God's idea of justice-mercy? International Justice Mission, a non-governmental organization, or NGO, fighting against human trafficking, not only pursues traffickers with focus and dedication but also prays that they will be healed and treated fairly in the justice system. In a commentary lecture on the Gospel of Matthew, Thomas Aquinas wrote, "Mercy without justice is the mother of dissolution; justice without mercy is cruelty." By dissolution, he is referring to debauchery and lawlessness. We could add to this that justice without mercy and mercy without justice are two approaches that fail as social solutions because they do not reflect God's character and good design for us. It is also worth noting that our efforts toward justice and against injustice do not simply involve physical needs. In her booklet, *Love Your Neighbor*, author Kathryn Feliciano notes that the work of justice and mercy is also about the restoration of relationships.[3] Our efforts must recognize that those we seek to serve are whole

---

2. Timothy Keller, *Generous Justice: How God's Grace Makes Us Just* (New York: Dutton, 2012), 44.

3. Kathryn Feliciano. *Love Your Neighbor: Restoring Dignity, Breaking the Cycle of Poverty* (McLean: The Institute for Faith, Work, and Economics, 2016).

people – body and spirit — with thoughts, emotions, hopes, and dreams.

An important consideration as we think about our call to be people of justice and mercy, is the corresponding call not to be people of hatred, vengeance, or retaliation. The Bible is very clear on this point. In our frustration or sense of personal hurt, it is tempting to lash out in response to injustice. It is tempting to become hateful or spiteful toward those who have done wrong. The Apostle Paul writes in Romans 12:19, "Beloved, never avenge yourselves, but leave it to the wrath of God, for it is written, 'Vengeance is mine, I will repay, says the Lord.'" This is strong language from Paul. We are not to be retaliatory people. Despite the temptation to retaliate and seek vengeance on a personal level, scripture calls us to be known for our love in word and deed. In his book, *Strength to Love*, Martin Luther King, Jr. wrote, "In spite of the fact that the law of revenge solves no social problems, men continue to follow its disastrous leading. History is cluttered with the wreckage of nations and individuals that pursued this self-defeating path."[4]

Why does God reserve the right to repay? For one, sin and injustice are first and foremost offenses against him and his good design and desires for humanity. Although we may be victims or otherwise impacted by injustice, God is the most offended. Second, God is the only one with an

---

4. Martin Luther King, Jr., *Strength to Love* (New York: Harper and Row, 1963), 42.

eternal, infinite view of things. Our attempts at vengeance and retaliation would only have imperfect results. As Dr. King pinpoints in the quote above, revenge starts us on a path that leaves a wake of trouble because it tends to escalate into a back-and-forth pattern of mistrust and hatred. Do not misunderstand Romans 12:19 or Dr. King's message. While we are not called to be people of vengeance or retaliation, we are called to be people of justice. We are called to bring healing and restoration to broken relationships, whether in the home, the church, the neighborhood, or the broader society. As Ambassadors of Christ, we are to work toward the flourishing of all of God's image-bearers. Fortunately, God does not send us into this work blindly or without direction. He has provided his Word which is the lamp to our feet and the light to our path, even as we step into challenging areas. We do not have to be limited by the ideologies and biases of the world around us. Instead, we have God's Word as the authoritative guide and source of wisdom by which we can navigate the intricacies of justice and mercy by his design.

Now, while we are parked here on this topic, it is important to make an important distinction between personal vengeance and societal justice while also integrating the idea of vocation. There are times that the systems of society must hold people accountable for crimes and unjust acts. Some people will find themselves called to serve in this area as a matter of vocation — lawyers, judges, police officers, those who serve in the military. These officials are, or at least should be, accountable to the law and the people of the nation. Christians working in these fields have the unique opportunity and responsibility to reflect God's good design and desires by never letting the temptation toward personal vengeance taint the need for societal justice.

    The call to do justice and love mercy is not a task. It is a lifestyle. It is a transformed mindset (Romans 12:1-2) that leads to an outward, publicly lived life marked by the pursuit of justice and mercy. We are called to do justice and love mercy in every realm of life — at work, in the church, in our homes, in our neighborhood, and in the broader society. What does this look like? At work, we are called to be diligent (Proverbs 13:4), honest (Proverbs 12:22), and trustworthy (Proverbs 11:13). At home, we are called to honor our father and mother (Ephesians 6:1-3) and not to exasperate our children but to raise them in the fear and admonition of the Lord (Proverbs 22:6; Ephesians 6:4). In the church, we are called to confess our sins to one another (James 5:16) and to correct a wayward brother in love (Galatians 6:1). When we have conflicts inside the church, Jesus gives us the most excellent way of resolving them in Matthew 18:15-21. As members of the wider society, we are called to love the sojourner, immigrant, orphan, and widow (Deuteronomy 10:19; Isaiah 1:17; Hebrews 13:1-3). We are called to submit to authority (Romans 13:1-7; Hebrews 13:17) and work for the welfare of the city (Jeremiah 29:7). Understanding each of these individual callings through the lens of Micah 6:8 forms a picture of the kind of people we are made to be.

    When we read these callings, we might initially see them as burdens, or as a heavy load placed on our backs. Remember from chapters 5 and 6 that Jesus invites us to be under his yoke, which is easy and light (Matthew 11:29-30). We are the beast plowing the field and he is the farmer steering us along. Together we are forming straight furrows. Our joy is to be with him, working in partnership with him, and co-cultivating the land. Pursuing godly justice and mercy is one of the ways that we follow Christ. To follow Jesus and to be imitators of God (Ephesians 5:1) is not a burden when understood from the point of view of a "transformed mind" (Romans 12:2). Instead, it is the best and only way for us — and the world around us — to flourish. In Christ, we can have hope in the face of injustice and unmerciful treatment because we know that he has already suffered, in our place, the greatest injustice in history and that he is actively working to make all things new (Revelation 21:5).

## SCRIPTURE READINGS

For the Lord your God is God of gods and Lord of lords, the great, the mighty, and the awesome God, who is not partial and takes no bribe. He executes justice for the fatherless and the widow, and loves the sojourner, giving him food and clothing. – Deuteronomy 10:17-18

Blessed is he whose help is the God of Jacob, whose hope is in the Lord his God, who made heaven and earth, the sea, and all that is in them, who keeps faith forever; who executes justice for the oppressed, who gives food to the hungry. The Lord sets the prisoners free; the Lord opens the eyes of the blind. The Lord lifts up those who are bowed down; the Lord loves the righteous. The Lord watches over the sojourners; he upholds the widow and the fatherless, but the way of the wicked he brings to ruin. – Psalm 146:5-9

Open your mouth for the mute, for the rights of all who are destitute. – Proverbs 31:8

Wash yourselves; make yourselves clean; remove the evil of your deeds from before my eyes; cease to do evil, learn to do good; seek justice, correct oppression; bring justice to the fatherless, plead the widow's cause. – Isaiah 1:16-17

Thus says the Lord: Do justice and righteousness, and deliver from the hand of the oppressor him who has been robbed. And do no wrong or violence to the resident alien, the fatherless, and the widow, nor shed innocent blood in this place. – Jeremiah 22:3

He has shown you, O mortal, what is good. And what does the Lord require of you? To act justly and to love mercy and to walk humbly with your God. – Micah 6:8 (NIV)

Do not oppress the widow or the fatherless, the foreigner or the poor. Do not plot evil against each other. – Zechariah 7:10

Blessed are the merciful, for they shall receive mercy. – Matthew 5:7

"For I was hungry and you gave me food, I was thirsty and you gave me drink, I was a stranger and you welcomed me, I was naked and you clothed me, I was sick and you visited me, I was in prison and you came to me. Then the righteous will answer him, saying, 'Lord, when did we see you hungry and feed you, or thirsty and give you drink? And when did we see you a stranger and welcome you, or naked and clothe you? And when did we see you sick or in prison and visit you?' And the King will answer them, 'Truly, I say to you, as you did it to one of the least of these my brothers, you did it to me.'" – Matthew 25:35-40

Be merciful, even as your Father is merciful. – Luke 6:36

He said also to the man who had invited him, "When you give a dinner or a banquet, do not invite your friends or your brothers or your relatives or rich neighbors, lest they also invite you in return and you be repaid. But when you give a feast, invite the poor, the crippled, the lame, the blind, and you will be blessed, because they cannot repay you. For you will be repaid at the resurrection of the just." – Luke 14:12-14

Beloved, never avenge yourselves, but leave it to the wrath of God, for it is written, "Vengeance is mine, I will repay, says the Lord." – Romans 12:19

Let brotherly love continue. Do not neglect to show hospitality to strangers, for thereby some have entertained angels unawares. Remember those who are in prison, as though in prison with them, and those who are mistreated, since you also are in the body. – Hebrews 13:1-3

If a brother or sister is poorly clothed and lacking in daily food, and one of you says to them, "Go in peace, be warmed and filled," without giving them the things needed for the body, what good is that? So also faith by itself, if it does not have works, is dead. —James 2:15-17

## DISCUSSION QUESTIONS

1. In your life, have you experienced justice without mercy? In other words, what is something you have done that deserved punishment — and got it — but for which there was little or no mercy? Explain.

2. Conversely, when in your life have you experienced mercy without justice? Or what is something you have done that deserved punishment but you "got away with it"? Explain.

3. How does it make you feel when you learn that someone else got away with something without punishment?

4. What are some examples of justice and mercy that are good and right in the eyes of the world but are out of alignment with God's good design and desires for humanity?

5. Perspective matters. Over time, our perceptions change with respect to the most significant injustices in society. With the progression of time, we sometimes see historical injustices in a different light than in the

actual time of the events. Discuss some of the ways that perceptions of specific injustices have changed over time.

6. What role should the church, not just individual Christians, play in addressing injustice in the world? As you discuss this question, consider that the Western world has rapidly secularized in the last 150 years, and a large portion of the rest of the world does not recognize the church as a valid player on the world stage.

7. What role should governments play in addressing injustice in the world? As you discuss this question, remember that Christians hold a wide range of political views. And remember that this question can be the source of very heated debates. As you discuss it, be careful about your heart posture toward those with whom you disagree. Remember that although you may disagree with them, they are image-bearers of God with inherent dignity.

8. There is a long history of Christian persecution in the world. For example, tradition holds that nearly all the Apostles were martyred for their faith. More recently, it is estimated that 20 percent of North Korean Christians are held in concentration camps, and roughly 1,200 are killed each year. Between 1991 and 2011, churches across Iraq were burned or bombed, and the number of Christians in that country has declined from 1.4 million to an estimated 450,000 or

less. In the United States, at least 42 black churches were burned between 1991 and 2021. In 2020, 10 predominantly white churches were burned in Texas. How should Christians respond to the persecution of the church?

# 9

# CALLED TO GENEROSITY

God is generous. He gives us life and supplies our every need (Philippians 4:19). He has given us his only Son as well as the Holy Spirit who indwells us. He gives us his Word, the means by which he reveals his plan of salvation and his desires for human life. If this were not enough, out of his abundant love, he gives us beauty, friendship, creativity, and community. He gives us each other by instituting the church as a worshiping community that works, serves, and lives together. In these and other ways, God is generous beyond our understanding.

In his book, *The Prodigal God*, Tim Keller explains that the word *prodigal* means extravagant. In the story of the prodigal son, we often understand the wayward son to be the extravagant one. It turns out, it is the father that is extravagant. Tim Keller writes, "The father's welcome to the repentant son was literally reckless, because he refused to 'reckon' or count his sin against him or demand repayment. [...] Jesus is showing us the God of Great Expenditure, who is nothing if not prodigal toward us, his children. God's reckless grace is our greatest hope, a life-changing experience."[1] Throughout the Bible, we see that God is radically generous and that we are called to be radically generous as well. Challenging as it may be, we are called not to do generous acts from time to time, but to *be* generous by living generous lives.

To understand generosity, we must once again turn to scripture. First, it is imperative that we understand that God owns it all. Psalm 24:1 says, "The earth is the Lord's and the fullness thereof, the world and those who dwell therein." In Haggai 2, God declared he would rebuild the temple, which would require great riches. To comfort the people, God said in v. 8, "The silver is mine, and the gold is mine, declares the Lord of hosts." God owns it all, including you and me. The Apostle Paul tells us in I Corinthians 6:19-20, "Or do you not know that your body is a temple of the Holy Spirit within you, whom you have from God? You are not your own, for you were bought with a price. So, glorify God in your body."

God owns it all. Everything in Creation is His, even us. Every human being belongs to God, not to themselves. God is the owner, and we are his stewards. The parable of the talents in Matthew 25:14-30 gives a clear picture of our relationship with God in this sense. As you dig into your call to generosity, begin with this

---

1. Timothy Keller, *The Prodigal God: Recovering the Heart of the Christian Faith* (New York: Dutton, 2008), xv.

truth: you are a steward of what God has given to you. God has designed the world in a way that flourishing is increased when we share generously with one another. Generosity is part of our call to serve. It is worth noting here that this view of generosity sheds new light on hoarding and theft, both of which are condemned in scripture. The 8th Commandment, "thou shall not steal," is not simply a charge not to take things that are not yours. It is a charge not to rearrange the allocation of material things God has given to each steward. We are to steward what God has allocated to us and let other stewards take care of what has been allocated to them.

To understand generosity, we also must consider that our hearts become attached to possessions. Jesus tells us in the Sermon on the Mount, "For where your treasure is, there your heart will be also" (Matthew 6:21). In our selfishness, together with the world's "wisdom" about possessions, we become very attached to things. Our status among friends and in broader society is often defined by our wealth and possessions — or at least the image of these things that we try to project. In the modern world, one's social class is very closely linked to one's wealth. This can cause us to forget that God is the true owner of everything. Deuteronomy 8:18 tells us, "You shall remember the Lord your God, for it is he who gives you power to get wealth, that he may confirm his covenant that he swore to your fathers, as it is this day." What an irony that we quickly forget this verse despite that it begins, "You shall remember…"

Matthew 6:21 lies in the middle of a larger segment in the Sermon on the Mount. In it, Jesus begins by telling us not to lay up treasures on earth (v. 20). He goes on to say that we cannot serve both God and money. Only one or the other can be our true God. The image we have is not of Jesus pounding his fist on the lectern as he delivered these words, demanding that we clean ourselves up so that we can make it to heaven. Instead, he concludes this section with words of warm reassurance. "Therefore I tell you, do not be anxious about your life, what you will eat or what you will drink, nor about your body, what you will put on. Is not life more than food, and the body more than clothing? Look at the birds of the air: they neither sow nor reap nor gather into barns, and yet your heavenly Father feeds them. Are you not of more value than they?" (Matthew 6:25-26). He is calling us into a profound and beautiful freedom — freedom *from* a life of anxiety and freedom *to* a life of generosity. With respect to possessions and generosity, he is inviting us into a life marked by a transformed heart and mind.

At this point in our journey of understanding generosity, it may seem that Christians should take vows of poverty and live without possessions of any kind. It may seem that God is calling us not to save for a rainy day or prepare for retirement. Let us go back to the Bible once again. The overwhelming message of scripture is not that Christians are called to live impoverished lives, but to live generously. They are to use their possessions and investments (and even their ability to make investments) to advance the Kingdom. In I Timothy 6:17-19, the Apostle Paul does not tell rich Christians to become impoverished but to get their hearts into the right place. He writes, "As for the rich in this present age, charge them not to be haughty, nor to set their hopes on the uncertainty of riches, but on God, who richly provides us with everything to enjoy." Similarly, the writer of Hebrews does not call for the abandonment of possessions but for the adoption of a generous spirit: "Do not neglect to do good and to share what you have, for such sacrifices are pleasing to God (Hebrews 13:16)." And, in Malachi 3:10, we find one of the most definitive calls to share a portion of our wealth in the community of the church: "Bring the full tithe (tenth) into the storehouse, that there may be food in my house. And thereby put me to the test, says the Lord of hosts, if I will not open the windows of heaven for you and pour down for you a blessing until there is no more need." This verse is not an opportunity to make a "health and wealth" deal with God whereby if we give a lot, he will give even more to us. Instead, he is saying that he has equipped his people to be generous and to meet needs through all he has given to them.

Generosity is an approach to life that, like many habits, takes conscious effort and time to establish. Ideally, our parents taught us to share when we were very young. But not every home teaches the virtue of generosity from a young age. For some of us, the mindset and practice of generosity must be developed after childhood when we take more responsibility for ourselves as adults. This often requires self-reflection and a willingness to consider what hinders our personal generosity. For example, we might believe that our income is too low to be generous and that we will be generous later in life once it becomes easier to do. Contrary to this approach, we have an incredible account in scripture. In Mark 12:41-44, we read that Jesus sat watching people put donations into a box in the temple. He saw a poor widow put two copper coins in the box, just a few cents. He told his disciples, "Truly I tell you, this poor widow has put more into the treasury than all the others. They all gave out of their wealth; but she, out of her poverty, put in everything — all she had to live on." What a remarkable story! Not waiting until she had more money, the woman gave out of her poverty rather than her comfort and wealth. To think that generosity will suddenly start later, at a point in time when it is easier, is fallacious and ignores the reality that the habit of generosity is formed over time with much practice.

Another hindrance to generosity is the perception that giving is someone else's responsibility. Perhaps we imagine that older and wealthier people are more responsible to be generous than the young. The reality is that everyone is called to be generous, each giving as God has enabled them. The tithe, which simply means *tenth* in Hebrew, has been the model of giving among God's people, regardless of income level, ever since Abraham gave ten percent to Melchizedek in Genesis 14.

Finally, as we consider our hindrances to generosity, we must consider that our wealth may simply be part of our identity. In a well-known story in Matthew 19:16-28, Jesus tells a young man that to be perfect, he must give all his wealth to the poor. Verse 22 tells us that the young man went away sad because he had many possessions. We do not know all that was going through the young man's mind. But we do know the result. Rather than acknowledging his own imperfection and accepting Jesus' perfection, and rather than jumping at the chance to follow Jesus and be generous with his wealth, he simply walked away. Rather than developing the heart and habits of generosity, we can also walk away by not responding to the needs around us.

What are some practical ways that we can live generous lives? First, we can understand that we are called to be generous with our money, possessions, time, and abilities. For many Christians, generosity begins in the local church. Supporting, with money and time, the local teaching and preaching ministry, outreach to the local community, and partnership in global missions is an important aspect of the Christian life. In addition to investing in the local church, many are called to invest in ministries and organizations serving the poor and underprivileged. As a challenge to the world's wisdom, Christians should see the time and effort they make at work as an opportunity for generosity. While we need to be careful about abusive employers, we must understand that our work is not simply an economic exchange of labor for money. As we will explore in Chapter 11, our work is one of the most important ways that we apply our gifts and abilities to the cause of human flourishing. As such, it is also one of the key places in our life to be generous with the gifts and abilities God has given to us. It would not be possible to list all the ways Christians can be generous in the church and beyond. In the discussion questions that follow, you will have the opportunity to explore and discuss some of the ways you think you might serve through generosity. The key is that we see generosity not simply as a periodic act of kindness but as a lifestyle driven by a heart posture transformed by the gospel.

God is generous and we are made to be like him. The generosity of one human to another is part of God's good design for flourishing in the world. In this beautiful design, we are called not simply to do a generous act here and there but to *be* generous with our possessions and time. We are called to understand that God owns it all and we are stewards of what he has allocated to us. We are called to understand that money, possessions, time, and abilities are given to us to advance the Kingdom of God, not to advance our own little kingdoms. Sadly, in our rebellion against God's good design, we hoard our time and stockpile our possessions. We easily believe the lie that our value and worth are tied to our social status which, in turn, is dependent upon our material wealth. It is also easy to believe that generosity is someone else's responsibility. In fact, we are all called to be generous, regardless of our stage of life. In his perfect design for us, God calls us to freedom from anxiety about what we have and to the freedom of generosity in Christ.

## SCRIPTURE READINGS

When you reap the harvest of your land, you shall not reap your field right up to its edge, neither shall you gather the gleanings after your harvest. And you shall not strip your vineyard bare, neither shall you gather the fallen grapes of your vineyard. You shall leave them for the poor and for the sojourner: I am the Lord your God. – Leviticus 19:9-10

The earth is the Lord's and the fullness thereof, the world and those who dwell therein, for he has founded it upon the seas and established it upon the rivers. – Psalm 24:1

Blessed is the one who considers the poor! In the day of trouble the Lord delivers him; the Lord protects him and keeps him alive; he is called blessed in the land; you do not give him up to the will of his enemies. The Lord sustains him on his sickbed; in his illness you restore him to full health. – Psalm 41:1-3

Incline my heart to your testimonies, and not to selfish gain! – Psalm 119: 36

And I will shake all nations, so that the treasures of all nations shall come in, and I will fill this house with glory, says the Lord of hosts. The silver is mine, and the gold is mine, declares the Lord of hosts. – Haggai 2:7-8

Bring the full tithe (tenth) into the storehouse, that there may be food in my house. And thereby put me to the test, says the Lord of hosts, if I will not open the windows of heaven for you and pour down for you a blessing until there is no more need. – Malachi 3:10

Beware of practicing your righteousness before other people in order to be seen by them, for then you will have no reward from your Father who is in heaven. Thus, when you give to the needy, sound no trumpet before you, as the hypocrites do in the synagogues and in the streets, that they may be praised by others. Truly I say to you, they have received their reward. But when you give to the needy, do not let your left hand know what your right hand is doing, so that your giving may be in secret. And your Father who sees in secret will reward you. – Matthew 6:1-4

For where your treasure is, there your heart will be also. – Matthew 6:21

"Therefore I tell you, do not be anxious about your life, what you will eat or what you will drink, nor about your body, what you will put on. Is not life more than food, and the body more than clothing? Look at the birds of the air: they neither sow nor reap nor gather into barns, and yet your heavenly Father feeds them. Are you not of more value than they? – Matthew 6:25-26

And he sat down opposite the treasury and watched the people putting money into the offering box. Many rich people put in large sums. And a poor widow came and put in two small copper coins, which make a penny. And he called his disciples to him and said to them, "Truly, I say to you, this poor widow has put in more than all those who are contributing to the offering box. For they all contributed out of their abundance, but she out of her poverty has put in everything she had, all she had to live on." – Mark 12:41-44

Jesus looked up and saw the rich putting their gifts into the offering box, and he saw a poor widow put in two small copper coins. And he said, "Truly, I tell you, this poor widow has put in more than all of them. For they all contributed out of their abundance, but she out of her poverty put in all she had to live on." – Luke 21:1-4

This point is this: whoever sows sparingly will also reap sparingly, and whoever sows bountifully will also reap bountifully. – II Corinthians 9:6

And my God will supply every need of yours according to his riches in glory in Christ Jesus. – Philippians 4:19

As for the rich in this present age, charge them not to be haughty, nor to set their hopes on the uncertainty of riches, but on God, who richly provides us with everything to enjoy. They are to do good, to be rich in good works, to be generous and ready to share, thus storing up treasure for themselves as a good foundation for the future, so that they may take hold of that which is truly life. – I Timothy 6:17-19

Do not neglect to do good and to share what you have, for such sacrifices are pleasing to God. – Hebrews 13:16

But if anyone has the world's goods and sees his brother in need, yet closes his heart against him, how does God's love abide in him? – I John 3:17

## DISCUSSION QUESTIONS

1. What are some examples of generosity you have seen in your life? Remember that generosity is measured

more by the heart of the giver than by the size of the gift.

2. What were the values and patterns of giving and generosity in your family? How do you think these patterns impact your thoughts about generosity now?

3. A generous life involves giving more than just money. It also involves giving your time, energy, and abilities. Which areas of generosity are easiest, and which are most difficult for you?

4. It is not uncommon for young adults to think, "I will start giving later in life, once I am more established." Do you agree or disagree with this approach? Explain.

5. Some Christians are committed to giving 10 percent (i.e., the tithe) of their gross income to the church. Some are committed to giving 10 percent overall to Christian work, only part of which goes to the church. Others have chosen a different percentage. What are your thoughts about giving percentages?

6. When two Christians come together in marriage, they sometimes have different views about giving and generosity. What is your best advice for a young couple beginning this sort of conversation and practice?

7. Is material generosity challenging for you? If so, what makes it difficult for you? Are you afraid of losing something? If so, what is that? What has hold of your heart in this area?

# 10

# FINDING JOY IN SERVICE

In the past few chapters, we have explored the idea that we are made to be servants. We serve because Christ is a servant, and we are made to be like him. We also serve because he invites us into a life of servanthood that, by his design, is for our good and for the flourishing of the world. By God's design, serving is beautiful and eternally profound. We are Christ's hands and feet (I Corinthians 12:27) that meet needs and show the love of Christ to those around us. Serving is a good — very good — part of God's design for us. It is a key part of the way God has designed community and human society to operate.

Looking back, we are reminded that Christian service throughout history is inspirational and encouraging. And yet, despite the beauty of Christian service, we often find ourselves hesitant. We sometimes fail to step in when needed. Given the beauty of God's design for us as servants, it seems illogical that we would not leap at the chance to serve all the time. Why are we sometimes hesitant to serve? Of course, there are many answers to this question: our selfishness and sin, fear, or lack of preparation. One answer worth our time and attention is that we have not learned to experience the joy of serving. Rather than having willing and eager hearts, we are often burdened by the obligations and challenges of service. In this chapter we will explore the idea of finding joy in servanthood.

Imagine that you want to host your neighbors for a backyard barbeque. You set up the games, buy the food, lay out the tables, and curate the playlist. You are imagining a wonderfully fun day filled with laughter and camaraderie. Preferences for introversion and extraversion aside, we could say that joy is one of the motivations for this event. You simply *enjoy* being with friends and neighbors and serving them this way.

Now, imagine a very different situation. One of your neighbors has fallen ill and needs help around the house. The neighbors on your street have decided to help him. They create a rotating service schedule for each family to take on tasks each week. The problem is that while this man wants the help, he is mean, ungrateful, demanding, and impatient. His tone is harsh and judgmental. He has strong preferences about how things must be done. For years prior to becoming ill, he let his home fall into disrepair so that few things work as they should. Fixing one thing means uncovering five new things that need to be fixed.

What is the difference between the first scenario and the second? In the first one, we are surrounded by easy people, doing something we love to do. In the second, we are serving someone who is at least hard to love, if not abusive. We will be asked to do things that are frustrating and of dubious value. In the second scenario, we will probably be, at the very least, somewhat uncomfortable. And here we start to see one of the reasons that we lose sight of joy in serving. Serving in the brokenness of the world is a direct reminder of the Fall. It is a reminder of human shortcomings. Serving in areas of real brokenness will take a toll on us. For these and other reasons, serving can be very difficult, but that does not mean there is not joy to be found in the service itself. The world often teaches that we need to take care of ourselves first and foremost, even as a prerequisite of serving others. In the world's value system, the airplane safety approach of "put on your own mask first" is applied widely. Biblical wisdom, on the other hand, calls us to be living sacrifices (Romans 12:1), to find our joy in Christ (Philippians 4:4), to be sustained by the Holy Spirit (John 14:26; Acts 1:8; Romans 15:13), to be equipped and nourished by God's Word (Psalm 119:113), and to be encouraged and equipped in the community of the church (Hebrews 10:24-25).

Another way that we can find joy even in very difficult service is to have a firm grounding in two important concepts of grace: *justification* and *sanctification*. Justification is the one-time act of God's grace in which the believer is declared righteous (Romans 5:1). Sanctification is the ongoing work of God's grace to set us apart for his purposes. It is a lifelong process of being conformed into the likeness of Christ (I Thessalonians 5:23). These two important words are often thought to mean the same thing. When we think about joy, or the lack of joy, and the call to serve, it is helpful to remember the distinction between justification and sanctification. When God calls us to repentance and enables us to have faith in him, we are justified. By his grace, God accepts us, once and for all, upon the merits of Jesus' death and resurrection. We cannot earn God's saving grace (Ephesians 2:8-9). Once justified, we can never lose his love or our place in the Kingdom (Deuteronomy 31:8).

What does this have to do with serving? While we can, by the ongoing work of the Holy Spirit, be transformed into more Christlike servants (sanctification), we cannot earn God's love by serving. As Martin Luther famously wrote in the hymn *A Mighty Fortress is Our God*, "our striving would be losing." Trying to earn God's love and acceptance through service is a really good way to strip service of its joy. In our limitations and fallibility, we will make mistakes in our efforts to serve. We will sin in our service. These may be very frustrating to us as we confront our shortcomings and the times in which we let people down. As frustrating as those situations may be, and as much as they are a call for us to ask for forgiveness, they will not take the love of God away from us (Romans 8:38-39). In our striving to serve perfectly and in our fear of failure, we sometimes deny ourselves the joy of service. Fully embracing the deeply wonderful and beautiful doctrines of justification and sanctification, however, we can see that we are truly free in Christ (Galatians 5:1). We are free from the fear of failure and of not measuring up, and we are free to give ourselves away to serve those to whom God is calling us, even if we fall short in our efforts.

With a proper understanding of justification and sanctification, we know that God's love is complete in us already. This knowledge gives us the freedom to experience the joy of service. And yet, we sometimes fail to experience that joy, not because we are trying to earn God's love, but because we are trying to please people (Ephesians 6:5-8). Perhaps more than in any other way, people-pleasing can be the thief of joy for the modern Christian. In trying to please everyone, we end up pleasing no one. Placing our focus on what people desire from us, rather than on what God desires, is not only unwise but a sure path to joylessness. Rather than giving someone genuine service rooted in God's design and desires for humanity, a people-pleaser may opt for the path that requires no confrontation even when correction and reproof are required (II Timothy 3:16). While this may be helpful sometimes, it is not helpful all the time. There are times when we are called, as part of rendering loving service, to confront wrongdoing and sin in those around us even as those same people expect us to accept them in their wrongdoing. People-pleasing will not only prevent us from serving in spirit and in truth but will leave us empty and joyless as we wrestle with it all.

What can we say to all of this? There is only one answer: Jesus *is* our joy. Our reputation and circumstances are not the ultimate sources of our joy. In fact, as we step out with a sacrificial, servant mindset, we are very likely to encounter very difficult circumstances. If our approach to work and service is rooted in God's character, we are almost certainly going to meet opposition and hardship from time to time (Luke 21:16-19). Despite these realities, we can find great joy in our serving simply because Jesus, our Rock, and our Redeemer, is our joy. Joy is not something he gives us that is separate from himself. He is the joy of our hearts. On more than one occasion, the

Apostle Paul found himself beaten and chained in Roman jail cells. Acts 16:23-25 recounts one amazing scene with Paul and Silas: "And when [the authorities] had inflicted many blows upon them, they threw them into prison, ordering the jailer to keep them safely. Having received this order, he put them into the inner prison and fastened their feet in the stocks. About midnight Paul and Silas were praying and singing hymns to God" (Acts 16:23-25). After being badly beaten and chained in the inner chamber of the jail, how could these men be singing? Even though they were suffering for their Kingdom service, they had an inner joy in Christ.

Most of us will never experience this sort of extreme suffering as Christians, and this level of suffering is not even the benchmark for good service. It should be clear to us, however, that there will be some level of suffering as we go about our Kingdom work. And, like Paul and Silas, we can find joy in our relationship with Jesus, the one who suffered beyond all suffering. We have the Word as the anchor of wisdom and joy. It is the balm of peace. Jesus is the Word incarnate who indwells our hearts and equips us for every good work (John 1:1-3).

Service is part of God's good design for us because it reflects his character. Since the world is opposed to God, we should expect to encounter resistance as we serve in God's name. We will serve hurting people who, in turn, hurt others...including those who are serving them. As we put all of this together in our personal service strategies, we must remember that Jesus is not a distant boss or an oppressive taskmaster. We are working with him collaboratively, in his presence, enabled by the Holy Spirit and guided by his Word. We must also remember that we exist in a liminal season between the Resurrection of Jesus and his return. Theologians sometimes call this period the "already, not yet." In his book, *Visions of Vocation*, Steve Garber encourages us to understand that in this liminal season, we must be satisfied with proximate, or imperfect, solutions.[1] The world remains broken, and our efforts fall short. We will not achieve perfection and yet we are responsible to serve, so we must accept that it will only get to be so good this side of eternity. Be encouraged! Living in Christ, equipped with his Word, we can find great joy in even our less-than-successful attempts at serving.

## SCRIPTURE READINGS

Only fear the Lord and serve him faithfully with all your heart. For consider what great things he has done for you. – I Samuel 12:24

Be glad in the Lord, and rejoice, O righteous, and shout for joy, all you upright in heart! – Psalm 32:11

---

1. Steven Garber, *Visions of Vocation: Common Grace for the Common Good* (Downer's Grove: Intervarsity Press, 2014).

Make a joyful noise to the Lord, all the earth! Serve the Lord with gladness! Come into his presence with singing! – Psalm 100:1-2

Rejoice in hope, be patient in tribulation, be constant in prayer. – Romans 12:12

Therefore, my beloved brothers, be steadfast, immovable, always abounding in the work of the Lord, knowing that in the Lord your labor is not in vain. – I Corinthians 15:58

We are treated as impostors, and yet are true; as unknown, and yet well known; as dying, and behold, we live; as punished, and yet not killed; as sorrowful, yet always rejoicing; as poor, yet making many rich; as having nothing, yet possessing everything. – II Corinthians 6:8:10

Each one must give as he has decided in his heart, not reluctantly or under compulsion, for God loves a cheerful giver. – II Corinthians 9:7

For freedom Christ has set us free; stand firm therefore, and do not submit again to a yoke of slavery. – Galatians 5:1

Bondservants, obey your earthly masters with fear and trembling, with a sincere heart, as you would Christ, not by the way of eye-service, as people-pleasers, but as bondservants of Christ, doing the will of God from the heart, rendering service with a good will as to the Lord and not to man, knowing that whatever good anyone does, this he will receive back from the Lord, whether he is a bondservant or is free. – Ephesians 6:5-8

Do all things without grumbling or disputing, that you may be blameless and innocent, children of God without blemish in the midst of a crooked and twisted generation, among whom you shine as lights in the world. – Philippians 2:14-15

Rejoice in the Lord always; again I will say, rejoice. – Philippians 4:4

I can do all things through him who strengthens me. – Philippians 4:13

Whatever you do, work heartily, as for the Lord and not for men, knowing that from the Lord you will receive the inheritance as your reward. You are serving the Lord Christ. – Colossians 3:23-24

## DISCUSSION QUESTIONS

1. When you are serving others, what types of service bring you joy? What is it about these things that gives you the most joy?

2. Talk about an example of service you have witnessed personally in which the servant was clearly joyful about the work they were doing? Try to use an example of someone you know rather than a general example.

3. Our motivation for serving can be complicated. Believers generally want to serve as an act of worship and to bring material help to those we serve. Sometimes, though, we serve because it makes *us* feel good. Talk about the ways you have wrestled with these complex emotions about servanthood.

4. Jesus suffered so that his joy might be made complete in us. He suffered greatly and yet was motivated by joy. As an image-bearer of Christ, how does his example inform your thoughts about suffering as a servant and finding joy in that service?

5. What aspects of serving make it difficult for you to experience joy? For example, maybe for you it is ungrateful people, frustratingly limited resources, or the sense that the task is overwhelming. Discuss these challenges and talk about ways that you have sought to find joy even when it is very hard to find.

6. Look back over your life and consider those who have served you — pastors, teachers, parents, friends, etc. With more mature eyes, is it possible to see that some of them found joy in serving you even though it was very difficult for them? What can you learn from them?

# 11

# WORK AS SERVICE

In this section on servanthood, we have been exploring the idea that we are servants, which is part of God's design for us as human beings. He placed Adam in the Garden to work it and keep it (Genesis 2:15). But why? Why did Adam have to work and keep the Garden? The Garden was a place of flourishing, a feast for the eyes and the stomach. By God's design, it produced food and shelter. And by God's design, Adam was an integral part of it. God created the Garden to need Adam as much as Adam needed the Garden.

As we have read previously in Genesis 1:27-28, Adam and Eve were charged with filling the *whole earth*, not just the geographic area of the original Garden. The Garden was perfect, but it was not finished.[1] In a sense, Adam and Eve were charged with making a place in which others could flourish. This is simply another way of understanding the Cultural Mandate. That mandate

---

1. Hugh Whelchel, *How Then Should We Work: Rediscovering the Biblical Doctrine of Work* (Bloomington: Westbow Press, 2012).

extends to us today. God's design for our work is that it is intended to benefit others. Like our first parents, we were made responsible for our earthly home and the welfare of one another.[2] Jesus came with this same mission. He veiled his glory and gave up the comfort of heaven, eventually giving up his life so that others might live. He was a carpenter turned rabbi (i.e., teacher) turned Savior. As we explore servanthood as an aspect of God's design for us, may we find a renewed sense of purpose and meaning in our daily work.

God's design for work-as-service is beautiful and complex. It is worthy of consideration that God's character is reflected in our work. Let us consider a few examples. Those called to the medical field are called primarily for what purpose? To heal. Bodily pain, sickness, and suffering are common to all human beings. Doctors, nurses, PA's, and others serve us when they do their jobs. Here is a remarkable thought: God himself is a healer! When we rebelled against God, bringing death, sickness, and corruption to Creation, God revealed himself as a healer that would bring new life and restore flourishing. For every person in the medical field, their work to bring healing reflects this aspect of God's character.

What about other vocations? Consider lawyers and others in the law profession. As you read this chapter, where is Jesus right now? He is seated at the right hand of

---

2. Steven Garber, *Visions of Vocation: Common Grace for the Common Good* (Downer's Grove: Intervarsity Press, 2014).

God (Romans 8:34; I Peter 3:22), ruling, reigning, and advocating for you and me. He is claiming justice on our behalf: "These are mine and I died for them. Justice demands that we never let them go!" People working in the law profession advocate for their clients to be treated fairly in the legal system and to benefit from a just process. Every day, legal professionals can have a special sense that they are reflecting God's character in their work because Jesus is also an advocate for justice.

We can apply this concept to every good work. Educators, did you know that the most common title for Jesus in the New Testament is Teacher? People in the sciences, you can know that God created a physical world that holds together in a sensible and discoverable way. In every good work there is opportunity to see that our work reflects God's character and good design. We can see that our work is a beautifully complex mixture of worship and service. Regardless of society's valuation of any given job, high or low, we can understand our work as part of God's good design for human flourishing. Martin Luther King, Jr. frequently borrowed an illustration from Benjamin Mays about work as worship and service. Dr. King said,

> "So we must set out to discover what we are called to do and what we are made for, and then after we discover it, we should set out to do it with all of the strength and all of the power that we have in our system. When you discover your life's work, set out to do it so well that the living, the dead, or the unborn could not do it better. And no matter what it is, never

consider it insignificant because if it is for the upbuilding of humanity it has cosmic significance. And so, if it falls to your lot to be a street sweeper, sweep streets like Rafael painted pictures. Sweep streets like Michelangelo carved marble. Sweep streets like Beethoven composed music. Sweep streets like Shakespeare wrote poetry. Sweep streets so well that all the host of heaven and earth will have to pause and say, 'Here lived a great street sweeper who swept his job well.'" [3]

We must also consider that in our work we serve by honoring the dignity of others. When we approach our work as service, we are demonstrating that we respect and appreciate those we serve, whether clients, colleagues, or other stakeholders. In serving others through our work, we convey that they are worthy of our time and energy. Some work is on the frontlines — providing direct service to others through medical care, mental health services, teaching, food service, etc. Other work is not on the frontlines but is service, nonetheless. For example, those who work in administration, finance, and information technology provide critical services to their organizations, colleagues, and ultimately to their clients. And, of course, most workers in the world directly serve their managers.

---

3. Martin Luther King, Jr. *Three dimensions of a complete life*. Sermon delivered at Friendship Baptist Church, Pasadena, California, February 28, 1960.

Business owners and executives cannot do all the work themselves. So, they employ others to take on some of the responsibilities. Within a larger organization, each person has roles, responsibilities, and expectations that reflect the value that person creates for their employer. Even in a very large and complex organization, each person can see how they fit into the larger structure. With eyes to see, they can understand that they are serving others, especially their manager, by contributing to the mission of that organization. As we work, we have our own roles and responsibilities, but our work combines with the work of others into a common whole. Understood this way, we can see that there is a beautiful diversity and interdependence represented in organizational work. We use things like smartphones or vehicles that we could not practically build on our own. We use complex services like health care and banking that can only be provided by a team. It is only through diverse interests and abilities woven together in an operating plan that an organization can flourish and serve its clients. With eyes to see, collaborative work-as-service is how the world is designed to be. Humans do not flourish alone. Instead, they are designed by God to work together for the flourishing of the entire world.

    It is good and right to reflect on these concepts with awe and wonder. What a God, that created such a beautiful design for the world! Despite its beautiful design, though, we are broken. At times, we may struggle with the idea of serving at work. Rather than seeing ourselves as a contributor in an array of people and organizations, we might feel lost, directionless, and unseen. We might lament that we do not have a bigger role, perhaps one with more influence and power. Even if we enjoy our job, we might be envious of friends who seem to be working in greener or happier pastures. At work, we are always with others who, like ourselves, struggle with the sins of greed and selfishness. Their sin and ours combine to make work much more difficult. Our sin robs us of flourishing. Rather than being excited about our work and the opportunity to serve others through it, we might consider it to be tedious, boring, and insignificant. How can we deal with these thoughts and feelings? The first way is simply to remember. God calls us throughout the Bible to remember who he is, what he has done and is doing, who we are, and that he loves us beyond measure — even at work. Grounding ourselves in these biblical truths is a balm for the weary working soul.

 A second way to manage our thoughts about serving at work is to acknowledge our own sins. Our natural tendency is to be self-oriented rather than others-oriented. The Apostle Paul calls us, again and again in his letters, to transform our hearts and minds to be living sacrifices (Romans 12:1). Without the humility of an others-oriented heart, we will struggle with servanthood in the workplace. We should consider this sort of heart change to be an essential area for professional development throughout our careers. A third way to manage our thoughts about serving at work is to gain perspective. When we turn inward, we lose sight of our place and our role at work. We lose sight of the fact that others rely on us and our contribution to the larger whole. Taking time each day to consider how our work "fits in" is a helpful discipline. The goal is not to convince ourselves of our importance. The goal is to remind ourselves that others are relying on us to do our part in the creation of goods and services that can only be created by a team working together.

Finally, a way to manage our thoughts about work as service is simply to keep going. Authors, Drew Moser and Jess Fankhouser offer this insight:

> "When we speak with [recent graduates that are now in their first jobs] the most frequent comment we hear is how they did not expect so many parts of their jobs to be so boring. No matter the industry, the mundane aspects of the work overshadow all the aspects they like. They often tell us they did not expect work to be so mundane, and it throws them for a loop. Some stay in the same job for years, putting in the same work, day in and day out. Others quit within months. So, what makes the difference? Hint: It is not that some twentysomethings are simply boring people, so they do not mind boring work; it's something much deeper." [4]

---

4. Drew Moser and Jess Fankhouser, *Ready or Not: Leaning into Life in Our Twenties* (Colorado Springs: Navpress, 2018), 107-108.

They go on to write,

> "It's Eugene Peterson's 'long obedience in the same direction' applied to work. Dogged, focused determination applied to good work makes all the difference. [...] When our work is unglamourous and mundane, we can quickly find ourselves holding back, saving our best selves for other endeavors. [...] At some point, we have to confront the question, is work the problem, or are we?"

As noted in Chapter 1, one of the most amazing things about the Christian life is that God is inviting us to be part of *his* mission and his work. He is calling us not to make names for ourselves or to be great in our own eyes, but to be humble servants, following the example of Jesus. What a glorious invitation! The challenge is to open our eyes and get to work, understanding that our work is one of the most important ways we serve God and others.

## SCRIPTURE READINGS

The Lord God took the man and placed him in the Garden of Eden to work it and keep it. – Genesis 2:15

Whatever your hand finds to do, do it with your might. – Ecclesiastes 9:10a

Even as the Son of Man came not to be served but to serve, and to give his life as the ransom for many. – Matthew 20:28

The greatest among you shall be your servant. – Matthew 23:11

Only let each person lead the life that the Lord has assigned to him, and to which God has called him. This is my rule in all the churches. Was anyone at the time of his call already circumcised? Let him not seek to remove the marks of circumcision. Was anyone at the time of his call uncircumcised? Let him not seek circumcision. For neither circumcision counts for anything nor uncircumcision, but keeping the commandments of God. Each one should remain in the condition in which he was called. Were you a bondservant when called? Do not be concerned about it. (But if you can gain your freedom, avail yourself of the opportunity.) For he who was called in the Lord as a bondservant is a freedman of the Lord. Likewise he who was free when called is a bondservant of Christ. You were bought with a price; do not become bondservants of men. So, brothers, in whatever condition each was called, there let him remain with God. – I Corinthians 7:17-24

Do nothing from selfish ambition or conceit, but in humility count others more significant than yourselves. Let each of you look not only to his own interests, but also to the interests of others. Have this mind among yourselves, which is yours in Christ Jesus, who, though he was in the form of God, did not count equality with God a thing to be grasped, but emptied himself, by taking the form of a servant, being born in the likeness of men. And being found in human form, he humbled himself by becoming obedient to the point of death, even death on a cross. – Philippians 2:3-8

As each has received a gift, use it to serve one another as good stewards of God's varied grace. – I Peter 4:10

## DISCUSSION QUESTIONS

1. Tell us about your career interest areas. That is, what fields do you want to explore in the next few years of your career? In what way will your work in your field be a service to clients, colleagues, and stakeholders?

2. In what ways will working in your area of interest be a challenge to you in terms of maintaining a servant's heart and mindset at work?

3. When we work together, humans can accomplish amazing things. Describe some examples of how this has been true in your life. How have you seen people work together, especially in the workplace, to accomplish great things?

4. It is easy to approach a job with the attitude and expectation of what it will do for you — compensation, prestige, excitement and entertainment, power, and control, etc. How have you seen these expectations

align or not align with God's design for us as servants at work?

5. In this chapter, it was proposed that we go into the workplace with the mind of a servant. What would the world be like if every Christian approached their work this way? How would things be different?

6. How can the church and smaller groups of Christians support one another with the challenges of seeing work as service?

7. Do you believe, in general, that Christians are more servant-minded than nonbelievers? Should we be? Explain.

# 12

# HE CAME TO SERVE

We have reached the end of the first semester of Roundtable conversations. Well done! We have spent a lot of time reflecting on the person of Jesus Christ — who he really is, not just who we want him to be. We are concluding the semester but also entering the Advent season. It is a special time to reflect on the coming of Jesus and his incarnation. He is the one and only *God-man* who uniquely and intentionally bridged the otherwise unbridgeable gap between God and humans.

This semester we have learned that God works, and that our work, in him, is good. In Colossians 1 and Hebrews 1, we learned that he is the One through whom all things were made and that he holds all things together. He is the one who is making all things new (Revelation 21:5). He famously tells us about himself, "I am the way, and the truth, and the life. No one comes to the Father except through me" (John 14:6). It has been our thesis throughout this book that life only makes sense when it is lived in relationship with Jesus. He made us and continues to sustain us in every way. The way we live matters because we are made to be like him, reflecting his glory and character. That is, we have important work to do. He invites us to join him in his work as co-creators and co-sustainers. It is good and right that we end this semester with a focus on the Advent of Christ and its meaning for us.

The word *incarnation* means "to embody in flesh." John 1:14 explains this idea elegantly — that God, the Word, became human and dwelt among us. In him is truth and grace, perfectly balanced and perfectly at rest. The incarnation of God is a beautifully complex mystery. How is it that Jesus is both God and human? How do his divine and human natures interact with one another? These are profound and glorious truths. While we may not be able to fully understand the incarnation, we can certainly grasp and understand its implications.

James Boice, the former pastor of Tenth Presbyterian Church in Philadelphia, suggests four important implications of the incarnation: 1) the incarnation reveals the value God places on human life; 2) it reveals that God has not abandoned us but loves and values us even in our fallen state; 3) it reveals that God is able to understand us and sympathize with us which, in turn, is a call to a life of prayer; and, finally, 4) Jesus in the flesh is an example of how we are to live.[1] God so loved us, John tells us, that he sent his only Son (John 3:16). Jesus

---

1. James Montgomery Boice, *Foundations of the Christian Faith: A Comprehensive and Readable Theology* (Downer's Grove: Intervarsity Press, 1986).

came willingly, veiling his glory and stepping down from the comforts of heaven to be with us, to live a human life, to die as a result of injustice, and to overcome death through resurrection. His appearance among us marked a turning point in history. God became incarnate, and nothing has been the same since — our sense of self and identity, our understanding of what it means to be alive, our sense of purpose and meaning at work and other spheres of life, and our hope for the future. And as much as we find answers to life's deep and difficult questions in Christ, the goal, the *telos*, of a life in Christ is not complicated. It is simply to love God with our whole heart, soul, and strength and to love our neighbor as ourselves (Mark 12:30-31). Or, as the Westminster Shorter Catechism asks, "Q: What is the chief end (*telos*) of man? A: To glorify God and enjoy him forever." Now that Jesus has come, we can be certain that God knows exactly what it is like for a human to pursue this *telos* and what it is like to face the temptations of a broken world.

In the late eleventh century, Anselm, the Archbishop of Canterbury, wrote a book called *Cur Deus Homo?*, which means *Why Did God Become a Man?* A thousand years later, this grand question is still worthy of exploration and meditation. To understand the answer, we must first understand that God is not bound by any laws or constraints. As the only self-existent being, the only one that can truly say, "I am that I am" (Exodus 3:14), nothing is above God. He *chose* to save us because he loves us, not because he was obligated by a higher moral law or law of grace. He chose to save us simply because he wanted it to happen. Similarly, he was not obligated to come to earth in the form of a man. He could have chosen any number of ways to accomplish his goals. But, in the end, he did come to earth as a man.

In response to his grand question, Anselm argues that the chasm between God and humans in their unrepentant state is infinitely wide. We are enemies of God (Romans 8:7-9) and dead in our sins (Romans 6:23). So, only God can bridge the gap to restore humans. To restore the relationship requires the power and reach of God himself. Yet, the gap is man's problem to solve; we caused it and are responsible for it. Adam and Eve opened the gap (Romans 5:12) by rebelling against God and we, in our own sin, carry on that terrible tradition. It is our problem to solve, but only God can solve it. So, Anselm argues, God chose the most perfect, loving, and gracious solution: that the Second Person of the Trinity would come in the person of Jesus Christ, God Incarnate, the Word become Flesh, fully God and fully human. Jesus alone was able to solve the problem of the infinite gap. As a human being, he could be held responsible for it. Jesus did what no one else could do. What beauty and what mystery! Therefore, Christmas is rightfully a season of joy, filled with celebration, feasting, and giving gifts to one another.

In the preface to his book, Anselm reminds his readers that although his answer to the question, "*Cur deus homo?*", may be elegant and cogent, we do not obtain faith through reason. Instead, he suggests that it is merely a way for the believer to be encouraged and to help others understand the gospel. We must remember that "faith comes from hearing, and hearing through the Word of Christ" (Romans 10:17). It is the Holy Spirit, not logic, that ultimately transforms hearts, taking people from death to life. It is the Word of God applied to our hearts by the Spirit that, in the end, does the work. In our salvation, it is not the elegance of the solution that we treasure, but Jesus himself. Jesus has come to set us, the captives, free. And he did not set us free and then abandon us. He came to be with us. He is Immanuel, God *with* us (Matthew 1:23). He invites us to be yoked with him in his work. He draws us into the *missio Dei*, to work in partnership as co-creators and co-sustainers of his Creation. In our work and service, we can find great meaning and purpose. And yet, it is not the joy, meaning, or purpose that we treasure in the end, but Jesus himself. Jesus is not a means to something else, such as joy and purpose. He is the end. Joy and meaning are simply things that come along with a deep, right relationship with him.

What can we say to all of this? Praise God for his most excellent solution that gives us nothing less than himself! Understanding all that has happened, all that it means, and connecting it to our sense of being and vocation, Christmas becomes a season of true and profound wonder. It is a season for us to bask in God's love and to rest in his grace. He has come at last! In the Advent of Christ, the beginning of the end of all brokenness is upon us. And the new course set for us is good, definitive, and irreversible because Jesus has come. In Advent, we can truly rest, not because we have finally found joy and a sense of purpose, but because Jesus has given himself. In him, there is true rest for our weary souls. In him, there is true joy. In him, there is true purpose. But even these wonderful things are only to be had *in him*. He is enough.

## SCRIPTURE READINGS

The Lord God said to the serpent, "Because you have done this, cursed are you above all livestock and above all beasts of the field; on your belly you shall go, and dust you shall eat all the days of your life. I will put enmity between you and the woman, and between your offspring and her offspring; he shall bruise your head, and you shall bruise his heel." – Genesis 3:14-15

For to us a child is born, to us a son is given; and the government shall be upon his shoulder, and his name shall be called Wonderful Counselor, Mighty God, Everlasting Father, Prince of Peace. – Isaiah 9:6

Behold my servant, whom I uphold, my chosen, in whom my soul delights; I have put my Spirit upon him; he will bring forth justice to the nations. He will not cry aloud or lift up his voice, or make it heard in the street; a bruised reed he will not break, and a faintly burning wick he will not quench; he will faithfully bring forth justice. He will not grow faint or be discouraged till he has established justice in the earth; and the coastlands wait for his law. – Isaiah 42:1-4

"Behold, the virgin shall conceive and bear a son, and they shall call his name Immanuel." – Matthew 1:23

And the Word became flesh and dwelt among us, and we have seen his glory, glory as of the only Son from the Father, full of grace and truth. – John 1:14

Long ago, at many times and in many ways, God spoke to our fathers by the prophets, but in these last days he has spoken to us by his Son, whom he appointed the heir of all things, through whom also he created the world. – Hebrews 1:1-2

But when the fullness of time had come, God sent forth his Son, born of woman, born under the law, to redeem those who were under the law, so that we might receive adoption as sons. – Galatians 4:4-5

But when the goodness and loving kindness of God our Savior appeared, he saved us, not because of works done by us in righteousness, but according to his own mercy, by the washing of regeneration and renewal of the Holy Spirit, whom he poured out on us richly through Jesus Christ our Savior, so that being justified by his grace we might become heirs according to the hope of eternal life. – Titus 3:4-7

## DISCUSSION QUESTIONS

1. What are some of your favorite Christmas traditions, and how do these traditions help you experience Immanuel, God with us?

2. A large portion of the world celebrates and embraces the Christmas holiday, but not Jesus himself. As a result, Christmas can be a confusing time for Christians, especially those who are young in the faith.

What are your thoughts about how Christians can celebrate the coming of Jesus even as the world has very different ideas about Christmas?

3. Anselm of Canterbury asked and answered the question, "Why did God become a man?" What is your reaction to his answer? Explain.

4. In the preface to his book, Anselm made the point that even a very good, logical argument will not help another person gain faith through reason. That is not to say that reason is not a good thing. His point is simply that salvation comes by faith alone in Christ alone, which is a gift of God. We cannot earn it on our own, even through very good logic. Discuss how this idea — that we are utterly dependent upon God for our salvation — sits with you.

5. The hymn "When I survey the wondrous cross" says, "Love so amazing, so divine…demands my life, my all." Now that we are halfway through this book, what have you learned about this? How have you grown in your walk with the Lord in this regard?

6. The greatest gift we receive as Christians is Jesus himself. It is easy, though, to think about the secondary benefits of a life in Christ as the things that primarily interest us — joy, rest, a sense of meaning. That is, we might be interested in a relationship with Jesus because he is the means to acquire eternal life or peace with God. In this sense, Jesus becomes the means to these ends rather than the end himself. Have you had this

"Jesus as a means to an end" thought at times in your life? What are the ends you have treasured more than Jesus himself? How do you navigate this in your walk with him and in your relationships in the church?

# SECTION 3

# COMMUNITY

God is One, and yet exists as a Trinity — Father, Son, and Spirit. He lives in perfect union and community within himself. As his image-bearers, God has made us to reflect him by placing us in community with one another.

When community is healthy and grounded in God's design, it is beautiful and restorative. Unfortunately, when we bring our selfishness, impatience, and other sins into our relationships, community can be the source of anxiety, grief, and heartache. Living in community involves recognizing and confronting brokenness while working toward something better — the Christ-centered flourishing of those God has brought into our lives.

This section explores several aspects of God's design for community. It is an opportunity to grow in love for one another, the church, and society in general. As with the previous sections, this is just a conversation starter. Take what you can from these chapters and apply it to your real-life communities. Let the chapters of this section be a starting point for much deeper conversation and life together.

# 13

# CALLED TO COMMUNITY

The need to belong is common to every human being. Even the most introverted individuals desire companionship, friendship, and meaningful relationships. God has made us for community. He calls us to live in harmony, serve one another, and work together toward the common good. We can see God's desire for community right at the beginning of the Bible. In the Cultural Mandate (Genesis 1:28), he commands us to fill the earth and to create a God-honoring society, a world filled with image-bearers working together to make something of this place that God has given us. Working together, we are called by God to have dominion over the earth. This is a responsibility all humans share. And we cannot miss the reality that Jesus came as a human being. He is Immanuel, God with us. He shares, perfectly, our desire to be in community with his people.

As we consider God's design for community, it is worth noting that the phrase, "God saw that it was good," is repeated throughout Genesis 1. Step by step, God completed his work of creating. At the end of each step, he looked upon his work and saw that it was good. Genesis 2 is a retelling of the Creation account from a slightly different viewpoint. In it, we learn that although Creation was good, God saw that the man was alone (Genesis 2:18). To make things truly perfect, he created Eve so that they could be together. They were meant to be friends, companions, and co-laborers. Adam and Eve were also in the unique relationship of marriage. In marriage, they had the responsibility of expanding the human family through procreation. This idea that man was not meant to be alone can be applied more broadly. God saw that it was not good for Adam to be alone *in general*. That is, God made Adam in such a way that he would thrive more with other people around him than he would by himself. He needed a family and a community. We still need community today. It is helpful to recall a point made in previous chapters: Adam and Eve were made in God's image (Genesis 1:27). God is one (Deuteronomy 6:4), but in a glorious mystery exists as a Trinity, three in one. The Father, Son, and Spirit exist together in perfect unity and balance. In creating humans, God reflected the community aspect of his own character. There is not a direct correlation between the human family and the Trinity, so we need to be careful in connecting the two ideas. But it is true that the community of humans, in a sense, reflects the community of the Triune God.

As we learned in Chapter 1, God is unfolding history in a Four-Chapter Gospel: Creation, Fall, Redemption, and Consummation. This story is playing out in the grand, cosmic sense. It is also playing out in the smaller scale of our individual lives and in the real, tangible communities in which we live. God designed us to flourish in community, working together for the benefit of each other. A tragic result of our rebellion against God is that human community was damaged. As we turned our focus away from God and toward ourselves, community became broken and corrupt. Like everything else in Creation, our sin left community in desperate need of repair. Marriages, friendships, neighborhoods, and society are all broken by our sin. Jesus, in becoming human, living a perfect life, dying a perfect death, rising to new life, and ascending to the right hand of God, has made the way for community to be redeemed in him. He has not only shown us the way but he has made the way. The Holy Spirit that now indwells us is sanctifying us and making us more and more into the likeness of Jesus (II Corinthians 3:17-18), which is our ultimate and only hope for community. By Christ's work, we can have peace with God and peace with one another (Romans 5:1, 12:18). While we remain in a broken world, we can be encouraged — and joyful — that upon Christ's return, our relationships with one another will be fully healed and perfectly restored.

As we await Christ's return, community can be very difficult. Genuine relationships require a lot of effort, and yet we desire them. Each of us brings our unique set of sins and brokenness into all our relationships. We annoy and hurt each other, intentionally and unintentionally. We put our personal interests before the interests of others, which is directly counter to the design God has for us. In our shame, we hide from one another and put on masks that prevent genuine relationships from forming. In extreme cases, we sometimes even oppress and abuse others in unspeakable ways. What a mess! The good news is that God is not silent on the topic of community and friendship. He has not left us to wallow in our brokenness. Scripture is filled with messages about God's desires for how we are to live with one another. In Chapter 15, we will explore many of these passages and the general concepts of what it means to have genuine love for one another (Romans 12:9-10), build one another up in the faith (II Thessalonians 5:11), carry one another's burdens (Galatians 6:2), and so on. In Chapter 2, we explored the biblical call to love one another. The ideas of that chapter apply here. You may find it worthwhile to go back and re-read that chapter as a reminder. God's call to love is so formative for us, so foundational to our character, that we can never stop learning about it. We must be lifelong students of love.

Community takes various shapes and forms. For example, there is the family, the small group, the church, and friendships beyond the church. Each community is unique in its purpose, structure, and dynamics. As we will explore in this section of the book, we are called to full participation in each of these communities. We cannot invest in our relationships at home while ignoring relationships in the church. We are called, after all, to be active members of the body of Christ (I Corinthians 12:27). We cannot invest in church relationships while ignoring our family because we are called to honor our parents (Exodus 20:12) and to raise children in the love and admonition of the Lord (Ephesians 6:4). We have a significant role in each of the communities to which we belong, and we are called to be Christ-like in each of them. We are called to love and serve even when that is difficult and uncomfortable. We must also recognize that the technology we are so tied to in our world today offers a promise of connection but often without genuine community. In her book, *Restless Devices*, Felicia Wu Song writes, "In our time of unprecedented connection — connection to people, connection to breaking news, connection to information and entertainment — one would think we would be satisfied."[1] Identifying the shortcomings of these connections, she offers a profound observation, "[...] most of us would admit that what we actually long for in our most intimate relationships is to know and be known, to trust and be trusted, and to experience the freedom in disclosing our most vulnerable and weak selves *and finding that we are still loved*. I think most of us intuitively understand this gap between connection and communion."

We must recognize that our communities shape us. We are formed and informed by the values, communication styles, and other preferences of our communities. In his book, *The Beautiful Community*, Pastor Irwyn Ince writes, "we are made in and for community and our understanding of ourselves is intimately tied to our relationship with one another."[2] As such, we need to be mindful of the ways those values and preferences align or

---

1. Felicia Wu Song, *Restless Devices: Recovering Personhood, Presence, and Place in the Digital Age* (Downer's Grove: Intervarsity Press, 2021), 107.

2. Irwyn Ince, *The Beautiful Community: Unity, Diversity, and the Church at Its Best* (Downer's Grove: Intervarsity Press, 2020), 54.

do not align with God's design for us. We are to be shaped first and foremost by God's Word more than by the world around us (Romans 12:2). In other words, we must remember that our identity is primarily found in Christ and secondarily in the communities to which we belong. At the same time, it is in and through community that we interact with the pluralistic world. Not everyone in our friend circles loves Jesus and wants to live by God's Word. Wisdom is required here. While we are called to love and serve friends and loved ones, we are also called not to be conformed to the world's thinking, ideologies, and value systems, perhaps especially where community and friendship are concerned. We are called to wisely discern between godliness and worldliness. To navigate these sometimes-challenging waters, we need to be students of community, understanding its forms and structures, seeing the ways we have been influenced and shaped by the communities to which we belong, and understanding our role in helping to shape those communities.

We have mentioned many times that Jesus is the center of life. There would be no life without him. It follows that he should also be the center of community. Seen this way, we can understand that all communities, regardless of their form, were designed for Jesus to be the central figure. He is the Lord of the home, romantic relationships, the church, and the broader society because he is Lord over all of them. We can look at his life in community as a model for us. He loved his closest friends dearly. He loved the masses that came to hear him and to be healed. He had compassion for those around him. He lived in a specific place and time and belonged to a specific family. He was the citizen of an oppressed nation. Many of those around him, including family, friends, and public leaders, tried to draw him away from his mission in one way or another. Even as he gave himself away so that others might have life, he never lost sight of himself or his mission. He loved everyone around him, but never lost himself to the local values or systems of thought. Despite his friends' desires that he would take over the government and become a political king, Jesus remained in his role as a humble, itinerant teacher and healer. Despite the many traps laid for him, he never took the bait. While the various communities around Jesus were trying to manipulate and discredit him, he kept loving and serving them as he had been sent to do. On one hand, he was the most genuine and committed member of any community in human history. He was never aloof or distant. On the other hand, he was never drawn away from God's design and desires either. Today, he stands ready to teach us about true community by his example. Let us learn from him.

## SCRIPTURE READINGS

And God blessed them. And God said to them, "Be fruitful and multiply and fill the earth and subdue it, and have dominion over the fish of the sea and of the birds of the heavens and over every living thing that moves on the earth." – Genesis 1:28

Then the LORD God said, "It is not good that the man should be alone." – Genesis 2:18

Behold, how good and pleasant it is when brothers dwell in unity! It is like the precious oil on the head, running down on the beard, on the beard of Aaron, running down on the collar of his robes! It is like the dew of Hermon, which falls on the mountains of Zion! For there the Lord has commanded the blessing, life forevermore. – Psalm 113:1-3

A friend loves at all times, and a brother is born for adversity. – Proverbs 17:17

Iron sharpens iron, and one man sharpens another. – Proverbs 27:17

Two are better than one, because they have a good reward for their toil. For if they fall, one will lift up his fellow. But woe to him who is alone when he falls and has not another to lift him up! Again, if two lie together, they keep warm, but how can one keep warm alone? And though a man might prevail against one who is alone, two will withstand him — a threefold cord is not quickly broken. – Ecclesiastes 4:9-12

For where two or three are gathered in my name, there am I among them. – Matthew 18:20

This is my commandment, that you love one another as I have loved you. Greater love has no one than this, that someone lay down his life for his friends. – John 15:12-13

For by the grace given to me I say to everyone among you not to think of himself more highly than he ought to think, but to think with sober judgment, each according to the measure of faith that God has assigned. For as in one body we have many members, and the members do not all have the same function, so we, though many, are one body in Christ, and individually members one of another. Having gifts that differ according to the grace given to us, let us use them: if prophecy, in proportion to our faith; if service, in our serving; the one who teaches, in his teaching. – Romans 12:3-4

I appeal to you, brothers, by the name of our Lord Jesus Christ, that all of you agree, and that there be no divisions among you, but that you be united in the same mind and the same judgment. – I Corinthians 1:10

That there may be no division in the body, but that the members may have the same care for one another. If one member suffers, all suffer together; if one member is honored, all rejoice together. Now you are the body of Christ and individually members of it. – I Corinthians 12:25-27

Do nothing from rivalry or conceit, but in humility count others more significant than yourselves. Let each of you look not only to his own interests, but also to the interests of others. – Philippians 3:10

Above all, keep loving one another earnestly, since love covers a multitude of sins. Show hospitality to one another without grumbling. As each has received a gift, use it to serve one another, as good stewards of God's varied grace: whoever speaks, as one who speaks oracles of God; whoever serves, as one who serves by the strength that God supplies — in order that in everything God may be glorified through Jesus Christ. – I Peter 4:8-11

## DISCUSSION QUESTIONS

1. Community life is relatively easy when things are going well and relationships are uncomplicated. It becomes more challenging when life is messy and difficult. Discuss an experience in which you failed to faithfully remain in community when things got hard.

2. Have you ever thought about community and relationships as a reflection of the trinitarian nature of God? With this understanding, community can be a worshipful reflection of God. Discuss your thoughts on this concept and its implications for life together.

3. How does the Four-Chapter Gospel (i.e., Creation, Fall, Redemption, and Consummation) inform your understanding of community life?

4. It can be easy to "check boxes" by going to church every Sunday, attending a Bible study, and serving in Christian settings. How can you go beyond merely being present to being genuinely invested in the lives of people that are part of the communities to which you are called?

5. How can you be part of and invest in your workplace community while not conforming to the pattern of the world?

6. Selfish expectations can be difficult to navigate in a small group. For example, someone with a deep desire for inclusion (or fear of exclusion) may be deeply offended if he/she senses a clique has formed within the group. Another group member may harbor unrealistic expectations about "pursuit" within friendship. Discuss with your group the impact of selfish expectations on group health and dynamics.

7. When you consider your small group, what are some ways you can be more Christ-like as an active member of that community?

# 14

# VULNERABILITY AND SHAME

God promises that we, as his children, will not be put to shame (Isaiah 54:4). Long before we were born, Jesus paid for our sins. Our shame was put on him at the cross. We have been spared. And yet, we often choose to live in our shame. We carry it around with us. It impacts our identity and our sense of self. Adam and Eve carried the shame of their sin but tried to hide under cloaks of leaves. Similarly, we often try to cover our shame in silly and useless ways that end up highlighting rather than covering it. Holding onto shame impacts all our relationships. By holding onto it, shame becomes part of our community life. The good news is that there is an antidote to all of this.[1] It is the grace of Christ and the life of vulnerability that is enabled by life in him. Rather than hiding in our shame or trying to cover it up, we have been

---

1. Curt Thompson, *The Soul of Shame: Retelling Stories We Believe about Ourselves* (Downer's Grove: Intervarsity Press, 2015).

given the grace to unburden ourselves through vulnerability before God and friends.

We all desire community. It can be like a woven fabric that holds us together. But what is it, really? What does it mean to be a friend rather than an acquaintance? The main difference is that you know your friends and your friends know you. With an acquaintance, interpersonal knowledge is limited and undeveloped. Friends know each other. Friendship is, among other things, a matter of tender knowledge. A community rests on the mutual knowledge of one another's quirks, preferences, strengths, weaknesses, and blind spots. In fact, the diversity of these things is what makes a community wonderful. Not everyone is the same — and the members of a healthy community know it. This range of interests, strengths, and weaknesses becomes the framework of how a community cares for its members. The diversity of gifts and abilities combine to make the community more effective than any of the individuals could be on their own.

Christians are not the only ones who understand the power of genuine community. The idea of membership and belonging has been studied and promoted by many others. For example, Abraham Maslow's famous Hierarchy of Needs includes membership and belonging as one of the highest-order human needs. He argues that knowing others and being known by them is an essential aspect of human well-being.[2] Viktor Frankl, a Holocaust survivor and psychotherapist suggests that all humans are on a grand quest, a search for meaning. Part of that search involves the "meaning of love." He writes of a person in a loving relationship with another, "By his love he is enabled to see the essential traits and features in the beloved person; and even more, he sees that which is potential in him, which is not yet actualized, but yet ought to be actualized."[3] This is a beautiful thought: friends not only see and know each other, but they see and know the yet-to-be-developed things in one another. In chapter 15, we will learn that friends not only see the undeveloped things, but they work proactively to help each other's development and growth.

We desire to know others and be known. That is, we desire genuine friendship and community. And yet, beyond all logic, we hide in our shame. We do not want people to see our weaknesses and failings. We want people to think our strengths and abilities are greater than they are. In our shame, we put on leaves and wear masks as we try to tell a different story of ourselves. In doing this, we hurt ourselves and the communities in which we live. How so? By hiding in our shame, we prevent others from truly knowing us. We prevent that "friend knowledge" that is essential to genuine love and community.

---

2. A.F. Maslow. (1943) 'A theory of human motivation' *Psychological Review*, 50(4), 370- 396.

3. V.E. Frankl, *Man's Search for Meaning* (Boston: Beacon Press, 2006), 177.

The trouble with masks and leaf coverings is that they do not actually work. God can see through them to the heart inside. Wise people can also see beyond the leaves because our coverings reveal something of what lurks below. A good friend can see when you are hiding something. We try to hide in our shame, but it has a way of showing through in our words and behaviors. Those leaves eventually fade, dry, and crack. They turn out to be much more fragile and transparent than we would like to think.

How can we change all of this? Digging into our shame will require vulnerability. That is, you will have to get personal. Most likely, it will also require a lot of serious introspection. What are some of the ways that you hide in your shame? What are some ways that you avoid vulnerability? Perhaps your leaf coverings involve competence and expertise. Maybe you need to be seen and respected as the most intelligent or informed person in the room and as a result, your thoughts and opinions are unassailable. Maybe for you, the issue is more about literal coverings, the need to be seen as young, beautiful, in-shape, or stylish, all to hide the insecurities you feel about your physical appearance. Perhaps you try to hide yourself in clubs and affiliations. Joining a sorority or fraternity during college, for example, can give the appearance of belonging while masking a highly comparative approach to life. Maybe you were "anti-sorority" or "anti-fraternity" during college and now wear leaves of judgment or contempt to cover your feelings of being an outsider. For some, the leaves can involve status and wealth. This can be particularly challenging for young adults that did not contribute to the wealth of their family and yet claim it as part of their own identity. Barry Switzer, the long-time football coach at the University of Oklahoma, famously addressed this situation when he said, "Some people were born on third base and go through life thinking they hit a triple." (*Note*: In saying these words, Barry Switzer was quoting an author whose identity is now lost to history). In the context of leaves and shame, we might modify his quote this way: "Some people were born on third base *but want others to think* they hit a triple." As you consider these examples and examine your own heart, you might see an important correlation. The relationship between our idols and our leaves is a near and dear one. We often use leaves to cover and protect our idols and those very idols are the things that do damage to us and to our relationships. Breaking this cycle will require us to get honest with ourselves and vulnerable with our friends.

As we have already learned, the antidote to this shame-covering mess is grace. It is a life of vulnerability that is enabled by God's grace. Rather than hiding in our shame or trying to cover it up, we have been given grace in Christ to unburden ourselves before God and our friends. In Christ, we are free to be our true selves. We are free to express that our identity is in Jesus, not in our strengths, abilities, or appearance. Rather than trying to be something on our own merits and then covering our shame when we fall short, we are offered a new way in Christ. We are offered the opportunity to be honest with ourselves and about ourselves. We are offered freedom not to abandon God's design for us by adopting the world's values in our lives but to embrace his good design. This freedom all starts with Jesus. Our freedom in him then extends to our relationships and to the communities in which we live.

Only as we live a real, genuine life in Christ can others truly know us. As we learn through the process of sanctification to be vulnerable and forthcoming about our limitations and failings, our communities become rooted in truth rather than appearances. We lose the burden of having to maintain those false appearances and leaf-coverings and, instead, can focus on the needs and well-being of others. Of course, even as we get excited about the wonderful possibility of this kind of rich community, we must remember the Four-Chapter Gospel. God is unfolding history according to his timing and not all things are repaired and renewed when we want them to be. We live in a broken world and in broken bodies that will not be perfected until Christ comes again. So, while we are increasingly transformed by the Holy Spirit, we will not get there fully until Jesus returns. Part of our work and struggle is to wrestle with this liminal reality, collaborating with the Holy Spirit in our own transformation while also waiting patiently for the completion of God's work in us and our communities.

In his book, *The Soul of Shame*, psychiatrist and author Curt Thompson suggests that we tend to think of vulnerability as something we do or experience from time to time. He proposes rather that humans simply *are* vulnerable. He writes, "[Vulnerable] is something we *are*. This is why we wear clothes, live in houses, and have speed limits. So much of what we do in life is designed, among other things, to protect us from the fact that we are vulnerable *at all times*."[4]

Although we are vulnerable all the time, most of us readily resist being or at least seeming vulnerable. In fact, some have suggested that even people who "overshare," those who seem to have no problem with vulnerability on the surface, are often monologuing to prevent others from asking questions and digging deeper. When we resist vulnerability, we fail to accept the grace we have in Christ, which brings significant consequences not only for ourselves but for our communities.

As students of community and leadership, it is imperative that we understand this dynamic of shame and vulnerability. We must confront these patterns in ourselves so that we might lead and encourage others to do the same, finding their comfort and identity first in Christ and second in genuine community. We cannot let our intolerance of discomfort prevent us from embracing the love of God in our own lives and in the communities in which he has placed us.

---

4. Curt Thompson, *The Soul of Shame: Retelling Stories We Believe about Ourselves* (Downer's Grove: Intervarsity Press, 2015), 120.

## SCRIPTURE READINGS

And the man and his wife were both naked and were not ashamed. – Genesis 2:25

And he said, "I heard the sound of you in the garden, and I was afraid, because I was naked, and I hid myself." – Genesis 3:10

I sought the Lord, and he answered me and delivered me from all my fears. Those who look to him are radiant, and their faces shall never be ashamed. – Psalm 34:4-5

But the Lord God helps me; therefore I have not been disgraced; therefore I have set my face like a flint, and I know that I shall not be put to shame. – Isaiah 50:7

Fear not, for you will not be ashamed; be not confounded, for you will not be disgraced; for you will forget the shame of your youth, and the reproach of your widowhood you will remember no more. – Isaiah 54:4

Behold, at that time I will deal with all your oppressors. And I will save the lame and gather the outcast, and I will change their shame into praise and renown in all the earth. – Zephaniah 3:19

For godly grief produces a repentance that leads to salvation without regret, whereas worldly grief produces death. – II Corinthians 7:10

Looking to Jesus, the founder and perfecter of our faith, who for the joy that was set before him endured the cross,

Vulnerability and Shame 171

despising the shame, and is seated at the right hand of the throne of God. – Hebrews 12:2

Therefore, confess your sins to one another and pray for one another, that you may be healed. The prayer of a righteous person has great power as it is working. – James 5:16

## DISCUSSION QUESTIONS

1. Curt Thompson suggests that vulnerability is the antidote to shame. If that is true, why do you think people are so reluctant to be vulnerable and so reluctant to share with others the aspects of their lives that bring them shame?

2. What is your posture toward vulnerability? Do you find it difficult to share elements of your life story with others? What makes one setting (e.g., groups based on age, gender, life experience) more comfortable than another for you? For example, some people are more vulnerable with their peers because they do not trust or want to disappoint their elders.

3. We use specific language to describe shame and vulnerability. For example, we might say, "I *feel* ashamed" or "I *feel* vulnerable." Contrary to the language, we are vulnerable, and Jesus has taken our shame. How do you sort through the difference

between the emotions associated with shame and vulnerability and the reality of them? Explain.

4. In history and various cultural settings, shame has been understood to be something passed from one person to another. For example, in Georgian England, a child born out of wedlock was likely to carry the shame of his parents' actions throughout his life. Or a child that did something bad might be thought to "bring shame on his family." How does this align or not align with the biblical concept of shame? What has been your personal experience with transferred shame?

5. If your group has been together more than a month, what discussion does your group need to have about vulnerability and shame? What would need to happen for your group to go deeper together?

6. Leaders, especially small group leaders, can often lead by example. What are some ways a leader can authentically exemplify vulnerability with their small group without undermining their leadership role?

7. Being vulnerable in a group sometimes involves confessing personal sins. Some Christians do this by dividing men and women into separate groups. What are your thoughts about this practice? Should men only discuss their sins with other men, and women with other women? Discuss.

# 15

## ONE ANOTHER PASSAGES

God loves us so much that he has not hidden himself away, leaving us to wallow and struggle in the dark. He has shared with us some of his inner thoughts and ideas. He gives these to us in the Bible, his special revelation to us. In the gift of scripture, God shares about twenty-five New Testament verses that we might call the "one another" passages. It is a collection of verses, dispersed over several books and letters, that, taken together, form a beautiful picture of what God desires for our community life. Because they are not side-by-side like the Ten Commandments, we might not know all of them or have them memorized. As we will see in this chapter, they form an important framework for Christian community.

It is helpful to remember that the "one another" passages are spread throughout the New Testament, and we must consider them within the various contexts in which we find them. While they are mostly straightforward and pithy statements that stand alone, a few of them are best understood only within their context in the Bible. It is also helpful to understand that most of these passages are quite general (e.g., "love one another"), but a few are very specific (e.g., "speak to one another in psalms, hymns and spiritual songs"). All the passages, whether general or specific, are given in the imperative, or command, form. A good practice in the Christian life is to receive imperatives within the context of indicatives. That is, it is helpful to first remember who we are and then to remember what we are called to do. The indicatives create a framework and foundation for understanding and applying the imperatives. As you read through these passages, take note that they are inherently "others" oriented. They are a reminder that our life together is much less about demanding our own way (I Corinthians 13:5) and much more about enabling others to flourish.

The one another passages are divided into two categories: 1) our general posture toward one another, and 2) specific actions we are to take with one another. The most general one another passage is "love one another." We find it repeated throughout the New Testament as a reflection of the second part of the Greatest Commandment given by Jesus in Matthew 22:36-40. We can think of this as the over-arching ethic for life in Christian community. Jesus tells us, in fact, that the world will know us by our love for one another (John 13:35).

What is love and how are we to love? Both the Bible and the world offer answers to this question. Scripture tells us, for example, that God is love (I John 4:8). He is self-existent and is not subject to a higher law of love. He is not required to think about love in a certain way or to be loving according to some sort of independent love code of conduct. No, love is defined by God's character alone. That means, as human beings, we do not get to make up our own definitions of love. It means that love is not self-evident or self-defining.[1] As followers of Christ, we are to learn about love in the Bible and then practice what we have learned by the guidance of the indwelling Holy Spirit. In scripture, we find that love is meant to be genuine (Romans 12:9), patient, undemanding, self-sacrificing (Romans 12:1), and rooted in the truth (Romans 13:6) — in other words, true love is reflective of God's character.

Within the call to love, there are three general one another passages: 1) be at peace with one another (Mark 9:50), 2) be kind and tenderhearted with one another (Ephesians 4:32), and 3) live in harmony with one another (Romans 15:5). Taken together, these verses paint a picture of harmony and mutual respect within the Christian community.

Creating divisions, grumbling, quarreling, and stirring up controversy are all condemned in Paul's letters to the church. Rather than being divided against ourselves, we are called to be at peace with one another and unified. In his second letter to the Corinthians, a community that struggled with peace and harmony, Paul writes, "Aim for restoration, comfort one another, agree with one another, live in peace; and the God of love and peace will be with you" (II Corinthians 3:11). These verses pose a significant challenge for many of us in the church today. We have

---

1. Rebecca McLaughlin, *Secular Creed: Engaging Five Contemporary Claims* (Austin: The Gospel Coalition, 2021).

learned many ways of arguing and getting what we want. Worldly philosophy teaches a lot of tactics in this area: never take 'no' for an answer, never let anyone stand in your way, never back down. These are common phrases that the world considers practical wisdom for success. For some of us, our desire to get what we want is not rooted in conscious adoption of worldly philosophy as much as it is simply part of our personalities. We can feel compelled to make a point and then continue arguing long after the point has been made. We sometimes feel the need to be the devil's advocate in conversation, even though the last thing the world needs is for the devil to have an advocate among God's people. We bring up the same issues again and again, even sustaining arguments and discord over many years. To get what we want, we might have learned all sorts of tactics like not revealing our true motives or pretending to be onboard while working behind the scenes in a manipulative way. Sometimes, our competitive drive leads us to see others as adversaries that we desire to defeat on the argumentation battlefield.

 The "one another" passages provide the outward expression of the love that will demonstrate to the world that we are Jesus' people. Of course, implementing these passages in real life can be challenging. In Acts 15, for example, the Apostles and elders gathered in Jerusalem to decide very important ethnic and spiritual matters. There was a lot of controversy and disagreement going into that council meeting. Despite their differences, the council emerged with a single message for all believers in all the churches. Similarly, the "one another" passages provide a useful framework for us today as we seek to sort out our differences. They offer a godly approach to addressing the important issues of our time while honoring the dignity of every person involved. They are a reminder that we are called to always love. We are not called to demand our own way. Instead, we are called to submit to those in leadership and to one another. We are called to be at peace with one another and devoted in our relationships. We are to approach difficult discussions and decisions with humility, considering others better than ourselves. Rather than looking to the world for tactics on how to get what we want, we should be a light to the world, constantly demonstrating our love for one another so that the world might know that we belong to Christ. We will discuss these ideas in more detail in chapters 17 and 18.

In addition to the general "one another" passages, there are at least sixteen specific passages. There are too many to discuss at length here, so we will focus on just one as an example. You are encouraged to meditate on the others in your personal study time. All the "one another" passages are listed later in the chapter. Here we will consider the passage, "offer hospitality to one another without grumbling" (I Peter 4:9).

Throughout the Bible, we are repeatedly given the image of God's people feasting with him — in the Garden, at the table, at the wedding of the Lamb, etc. In addition, God makes clear that he has taken us in, adopted us, and made us heirs (Romans 8:12-17). Under the Old Covenant, God's people were restricted in the foods they could eat. This was a sign and emblem of their separatedness and how they were not to be like the world around them. Under the New Covenant, God opens the door to gentile believers and, correspondingly, to new foods (Acts 10; I Timothy 4). God offers broad and open hospitality even though we do not deserve a place at his table. Our sin is an abomination to God and offensive to him. And yet in Christ, he welcomes us with open and extravagantly generous arms. Clearly, we are called to be welcoming and generous as well. The opening of the table to new foods is reflective of the opening of God's table to all people. We are called to invite others and show them hospitality in our churches and in our homes. And yet we cannot miss the second part of this passage: that we are do this without grumbling. It is so easy and tempting for us to be hospitable just for show or out of feelings of obligation. To do it out of genuine love is much more challenging because our hearts are out of alignment with God's design for radical hospitality. To be radically hospitable, especially to those who are different from us or those we find hard to love, is to demonstrate a form of vulnerability. Recall from Chapter 14 that vulnerability is very hard for us and something we often try to avoid.

The "one another" passages, taken together, offer an amazing view into God's design and desires for Christian community. These passages apply at the micro and macro levels of life — in close friendships, in our small groups, and in the whole church. As you read through them, you may have found yourself saying, "But what about…injustice, righteous anger, difficult people? How can we simply love and accept people that are doing bad things?" God knew about all these things when he gave us the "one another" passages. He is calling us to work toward justice and mercy, *and* he is calling us to go about it in a way that honors and reflects his character. Whether these passages are easy or difficult for you to accept and practice, they provide a memorable framework of how we are to love one another. Why not challenge yourself, and perhaps your entire friend community, to memorize these passages? As we memorize and practice them, may God enable us to love and live out these verses to his glory. May the world know that we belong to Jesus because we love each other in these ways.

## GENERAL ONE ANOTHER PASSAGES

Love one another – John 13:34-35; John 15:12; John 15:17; Romans 12:10; I Peter 4:8; I John 3:11; I John 3:23; I John 4:7; I John 4:11-12; II John 5

Be at peace with one another – Mark 9:50

Be kind and tenderhearted toward one another – Ephesians 4:32

Live in harmony with one another –Romans 15:5

## SPECIFIC ONE ANOTHER PASSAGES

Agree with one another – II Corinthians 3:11

Bear with one another in love – Ephesians 4:2

Bear one another's burdens – Galatians 6:2

Build one another up in the faith – I Thessalonians 5:11

Comfort one another – II Corinthians 3:11

Confess your sins to one another – James 5:16

Encourage one another in the word – Hebrews 10:25; I Thessalonians 4:18; I Thessalonians 5:11

Exhort one another every day – Hebrews 3:13

Forgive one another – Ephesians 4:32; Colossians 3:13

Show honor to one another – Romans 12:10

Greet one another with a holy kiss – Romans 16:16; I Corinthians 16:20; I Peter 5:14

Instruct one another from the indwelling Word of God – Romans 15:14; Colossians 3:16

Look not only to your own interests, but also to the interests of one another – Philippians 2:4

Pray for one another – James 5:16

Serve one another in love – Galatians 5:13; I Peter 4:10

Speak to one another with psalms, hymns, and spiritual songs – Ephesians 5:19

Spur one another on to love and good deeds – Hebrews 10:24

Stop passing judgment on one another – Romans 14:13

Submit to one another out of reverence for Christ, especially those who are older – Ephesians 5:21; I Peter 5:5

Value others above yourself, doing nothing out of selfish ambition or vain conceit – Philippians 2:3

Welcome one another – Romans 15:7

## DISCUSSION QUESTIONS

1. The one another passages reveal God's desire for his people to be others-oriented. As you consider these verses together, what comes to mind about God's plan for you, for your community, for your church, and for the world?

2. On the surface, some of these verses might seem in conflict. For example, we are called to stop passing judgment on one another (Romans 14:13) while exhorting (Hebrews 3:13), instructing, and admonishing one another (Colossians 3:16). Are these truly in conflict? Discuss ways we can admonish sin without judgment?

3. Which one another passage is most difficult for you personally? That is, which one do you have practicing? Talk about why it is difficult for you.

4. On the surface, these verses imply a level of intimacy, trust, and friendship. And yet, we know that the early church had brand new believers as well as those that had been around for a while. We cannot assume that they all knew each other well. Talk about your own comfort/discomfort about being vulnerable when you do not know others very well.

5. What would the world think of the church if we practiced these verses all the time? Do you think the world would recognize the inherent goodness in these traits? Explain.

6. Putting together all you have learned so far in your Fellows program, how do you think the "one another" passages fit into the mission of God?

7. The one another passages do not come with qualifiers. For example, none of them start with, "When it is convenient" or "Once you get comfortable." These passages apply to our lives now and always. Do you sometimes give yourself a pass for the responsibility of living by these passages? If so, when are you most likely to do that?

# 16

# CALLED TO LIFE IN THE CHURCH

For the past two decades, a clear and steady trend has emerged that should grab our attention: the decline of church membership and attendance. In 2020, the Barna Group reported that 68 percent of Americans identify as Christian in demographic surveys.[1] When asked about the details of their faith (e.g., if they consider Jesus to be their Lord and Savior, if they consider the Bible to be the Word of God, etc.), the percentage of what Barna calls "practicing Christians" drops to roughly 25 percent among older adults and even lower percentages for young Millennials and Gen Z. When asked about participation in the local church, only 29 percent of Christians reported weekly attendance, which has declined by roughly one-third since 1993. Church hopping and church shopping have also been on the rise. How can we think about these trends? And how can we understand them considering

---

1. Barna Group, LLC. *The State of the Church* 2020.

other trends such as the rise of the megachurch, celebrity pastors, and various financial and sexual scandals among church members and leaders?

Before we can contemplate trends in the church at large, we need to reflect on our own hearts and attitudes about the local church. We need to consider whether our views of the church are shaped more by popular thought and ideology or by scripture. We need to honestly assess our tendency to hold the entire church in contempt for the failings of individuals that have disappointed or hurt us. We also need to consider if our views about our own attendance and investment in the local church are shaped by God's design for us or by our desires for ourselves. The recent trend among Christians and non-Christians is to critically evaluate the church as they would any other human institution, sometimes even calling for its deconstruction when it does not conform to contemporary values. Among Christians, this and similar trends often lead to the practice of shopping around for a church that is most comfortable or perhaps least uncomfortable. Even after finding a church, it is common to keep one eye on other churches to see if there are greener pastures that we might enjoy more. Sadly, those greener pastures are often defined more by what is popular, entertaining, and seemingly enlightened than by what is truly good and lasting.

Here is the burning question: Does God expect or require local church membership and participation? A lot of ink has been spilled on this topic in books, articles, and blog posts. The answer is a little complicated — basically "no" and "yes." There is no explicit command in scripture,

"Thou shalt be present and accounted for every Sunday." At the same time, there is significant evidence in scripture that, unless providentially hindered, active participation in the local church is a good and wise part of a healthy Christian life. On one hand, there is freedom in Christ that enables us to be flexible about church attendance. On the other hand, we are to be devoted to one another in the bonds of community commitments within the church (Romans 12:10). We are not to exercise our freedom in such a way that we fall out of the habit of regular corporate worship and active church life (Hebrews 10:24-25).

As an expression of commitment, formal membership in the local church typically involves a public statement of faith. In addition to a statement of faith in Christ, several denominations ask new members something like this: "Will you support the Church in its worship and work to the best of your ability?" and "submit yourselves to the government and discipline of the church, and promise to study its purity and peace?"[2] While each denomination has its own approach to church membership, community commitment-making and commitment-keeping are typically part of it. Active membership and participation in the church are good for the individual because the church is the unique community of God's people, called to love, encourage, and serve one another. Members can grow in faith, side-by-

---

2. Presbyterian Church in America, *Book of Church Order*, 57-5.

side with other believers, as iron sharpens iron (Proverbs 27:17).

It is worth noting that most of the epistles of the New Testament are addressed to the church rather than individuals (and even those written to individuals are meant for everyone in the church). These words of God, spoken through the writers, are intended for equipping God's people, individually and corporately. Properly understood, the New Testament was given to the church as a whole. The "one another" passages that we discussed in the previous chapter, when taken together, are words for the upbuilding of the church. They are a picture of God's design for our life together. Through the habit of meeting, serving side-by-side, and growing together, we are to invest in one another as the community of Christ, the Bride for whom he died.

If we agree that we are to be active members in a church, we must ask, what is *the church*? It is a unique institution, perhaps better described as a body, founded by Jesus to do the work of the gospel. It is founded upon the Lord Jesus Christ himself (Matthew 16:16-18), shaped by the heart-transforming work of the Holy Spirit (Acts 1:8), and destined to contain people of every tribe, tongue, and nation (Revelation 7:9). In Acts 2, people came together into the first church from many nations: Arabians, Cappadocians, Cretans, Elamites, Jews, Judeans, Medes, Mesopotamians, Parthians, Romans, and others. They were not just a collection of people marked by their differences. They were primarily marked by their shared faith in Christ. Their unity in Christ overshadowed their differences. In Ephesians 2:14-20, using the analogy of two people, one Jew and one Gentile, the Apostle Paul describes the creation of one new person, in place of the two. The hostilities that existed between them, resulting from many prejudices and injustices over time, are put to rest in Christ. Having emphasized the one body of Christ in Ephesians 2, Paul explains the work of the new, unified body in chapter 4:15-16: "Speaking the truth in love, we are to grow up in every way into him who is the head, into Christ, from whom the whole body, joined and held together by every joint with which it is equipped, when each part is working properly, makes the body grow so that it builds itself up in love." What are we called to do? We are brought together to speak the truth in love, grow in Christ, and work together as members of one body in the work of the gospel.

As we allow ourselves to come together in unity, our sense of identity is transformed. We are still ourselves, of course. In joining the church, we have not become lost like a drop of water in the ocean. And yet, our identity, individually and together, is now first and foremost found in Christ. The old has gone and the new has come (II Corinthians 5:17). God has brought us into the church so that we might be the hands and feet of Christ to the world around us (I Corinthians 12:27). Peter tells us that we, together, "are a chosen race, a royal priesthood, a holy nation, a people for his own possession, that you may proclaim the excellencies of him who called you out of darkness into his marvelous light" (I Peter 2:9). He has brought us together, making one church out of many people, with a holy purpose: to proclaim and demonstrate to the world and to each other the wonder and glory of

God! Our mission is to be a visible representation of God himself, image-bearers, fully engaged in the *missio Dei*. God has brought us together in Christ and empowered us by the Holy Spirit, to do his work — together and unified. Our personal faith in Christ does not exist in the isolation of our personal preferences. Our personal relationship with Christ only makes sense and can only truly grow in the context of the wider church community in which God has placed us.

Our personal growth is linked to the growth of the body. Our commitment to one another and our love for one another are reflections of our personal growth in Christ. Serving one another, leading, and allowing ourselves to be led, submitting to the authority placed over us in the church, working toward like-mindedness — these are all ways that the body grows as we grow personally. Wallowing in jealousy, grumbling, holding grudges, resisting the change of heart that comes from hearing God's Word — all these personal failings hinder the growth of the body. Clinging to selfishness is a personal failing that becomes an issue for the church. In a similar way, it is essential that we understand the inherent diversity created by God in the church. Individually, we have gifts, abilities, and life experiences that are unique to us. Together, those things become part of one body, unified in one mission.

In Romans 12:4-8, Paul exhorts us to identify and deploy the unique gifts God has given us for the upbuilding of the church. He charges us to use these gifts with cheerfulness and generosity so that others might benefit from them. As we reflect on the beauty of God's design for his church, let us embrace the role and responsibilities he has given each of us and not be tempted to choose a church based on comfort, personal preference, or worldly measures. Instead, let us invest in a local church and commit ourselves to its mission and the relationships that can be formed there.

## SCRIPTURE READINGS

Iron sharpens iron, and one man sharpens another. – Proverbs 27:17

Simon Peter replied, "You are the Christ, the Son of the living God." And Jesus answered him, "Blessed are you, Simon Bar-Jonah! For flesh and blood has not revealed this to you, but my Father who is in heaven. And I tell you, you are Peter, and on this rock I will build my church, and the gates of hell shall not prevail against it." – Matthew 16:16-18

For where two or three are gathered in my name, there am I among them. – Matthew 18:20

And Jesus came and said to them, "All authority in heaven and on earth has been given to me. Go therefore and make disciples of all nations, baptizing them in the name of the Father and of the Son and of the Holy Spirit, teaching them to observe all that I have commanded you. And behold, I am with you always, to the end of the age." – Matthew 28:18-20

But, you will receive power when the Holy Spirit has come upon you, and you will be my witnesses in Jerusalem and in all Judea and Samaria, and to the end of the earth. – Acts 1:8

For as in one body we have many members, and the members do not all have the same function, so we, though many, are one body in Christ, and individually members one of another. Having gifts that differ according to the grace given to us, let us use them: if prophecy, in proportion to our faith; if service, in our serving; the one who teaches, in his teaching; the one who exhorts, in his exhortation; the one who contributes, in generosity; the one who leads, with zeal; the one who does acts of mercy, with cheerfulness. – Romans 12:4-8

Be devoted to one another in love. Honor one another above yourselves. – Romans 12:10 (NIV)

Now you are the body of Christ and individually members of it. – I Corinthians 12:27

For he himself is our peace, who has made us both one and has broken down in his flesh the dividing wall of hostility by abolishing the law of commandments expressed in ordinances, that he might create in himself one new man in place of the two, so making peace, and might reconcile us both to God in one body through the cross, thereby killing the hostility. And he came and preached peace to you who were far off and peace to those who were near. For through him we both have access in one Spirit to the Father. So then you are no longer strangers and aliens, but you are fellow citizens with the saints and members of the household of God, built on the foundation of the apostles and prophets, Christ Jesus himself being the cornerstone, in whom the whole structure, being joined together, grows into a holy temple in the Lord. – Ephesians 2:14-21

Now I rejoice in my sufferings for your sake, and in my flesh I am filling up what is lacking in Christ's afflictions for the sake of his body, that is, the church, of which I became a minister according to the stewardship from God that was given to me for you, to make the word of God fully known, the mystery hidden for ages and generations but now revealed to his saints. To them God chose to make known how great among the Gentiles are the riches of the glory of this mystery, which is Christ in you, the hope of glory. – Colossians 1:24-27

And let us consider how to stir up one another to love and good works, not neglecting to meet together, as is the habit of some, but encouraging one another, and all the more as you see the Day drawing near. – Hebrews 10:24-25

Obey your leaders and submit to them, for they are keeping watch over your souls, as those who will have to give an account. Let them do this with joy and not with groaning, for that would be of no advantage to you. – Hebrews 13:17

But, you are a chosen race, a royal priesthood, a holy nation, a people for his own possession, that you may proclaim the excellencies of him who called you out of darkness into his marvelous light. – I Peter 2:9

After this I looked, and behold, a great multitude that no one could number, from every nation, from all tribes and peoples and languages, standing before the throne and before the Lamb, clothed in white robes, with palm branches in their hands. – Revelation 7:9

## DISCUSSION QUESTIONS

1. What has your experience been of the church in the various seasons of your life — as a child, an adolescent, a college student, etc.? How have these experiences formed your vision of the church today?

2. Jesus loves the church and calls us, his followers, to be active parts of it. How does this calling sit with you? Do you accept the call to be an active member of the local church body, or do you reject it? On what do you base your view?

3. Jesus died out of love for his bride, the church. He has never stopped loving the church. Do you agree? Would you say that your love for the church is informed by his? Talk about the idea that his call on you to be an active part of the local church is part of his love for you and for the local church.

4. When we become Christians, our identity is first and foremost in Christ. What are some of the ways that we resist this teaching from the Bible? How can we be respectful of the elements of identity that separate us,

while also holding fully to the idea that we are first and foremost unified in Christ at the level of identity?

5. What are some ways that you are most excited about being active in the local church? How do you anticipate applying your gifts to the work and ministries of the local church? Why are you looking forward to these things? How do you think it will impact your relationships in the church?

6. If there was one thing you could say to a teenager who is struggling to be committed to their local church, what would it be? How would you encourage that teenager with Hebrews 10:24-25?

7. In our time, it is tempting to see the church more for its flaws and missteps than as the beloved bride of Christ. We might find ourselves harboring thoughts like, "I love Christ, but I do not love Christians." How can we encourage those that have such thoughts?

8. In many ways the world does not love the church. Books and movies often portray the church in a negative light. Do these worldly influences impact your views of the church? To what extent are your thoughts about the church more informed by the world's views than by Scripture? Discuss.

# 17

# PEACEMAKING

Sadly, conflict among humans, even followers of Christ, is very common. We find ourselves living in discord and disagreeing more often than most of us would like. From the little squabbles that set us off to the major differences that break us apart, conflict is part of life in a broken world. Little conflicts can ruin a family dinner, a business meeting, or a party. Sustained conflict within friendships, churches, and families can have devastating impacts for many years and over generations if healing and reconciliation are not pursued faithfully. Some human conflict, especially when rooted in patterns of abuse, goes unresolved this side of eternity.

In our conflicts, small and large, there is often hurt and pain for everyone involved. Consequently, there is also not much flourishing in those situations. Rather than resolving our conflicts, some of us choose to avoid them while harboring ill feelings toward others or gossiping about them within seemingly safe circles. It is very easy to find ourselves talking with "our people" about "those people." On the other hand, some of us cannot resist the temptation of jumping into open conflict a bit too willingly, often with disregard for better judgment and true peace-seeking.

In his Word, God provides a better way. Scripture is clear that we are to be working toward peace with one another, even when it is very difficult to achieve. And we are called to be people of grace, forgiving, and accepting one another even in our most obvious faults. As the hands and feet of Jesus, we are called to be peacemakers, bringing reconciliation and the reestablishment of right relationships. To this end, Pastor Irwyn Ince poses a profound challenge to us, "The world should look at the church in amazement and wonder, 'How did this happen?' 'How did people with such differences come together and commit to staying together in spite of the difficulty?'"[1]

Why is there so much conflict between us? Why are there so many verses in the Bible about it? As we have seen in previous chapters, it all goes back to the fall of mankind. We are designed to live for God's glory and the building up of a God-honoring, others-oriented society. And yet, in our recurring pattern of sin, we focus on ourselves and act in ways that cause deep divisions. Rather than seeking true reconciliation, we far too often demand our own version of justice.

Recall Romans 12 in which the Apostle Paul calls us to no longer conform to the pattern of the world but to renew our minds in Christ. He gives this command

---

1. Irwyn Ince, *The Beautiful Community: Unity, Diversity, and the Church at Its Best* (Downer's Grove: Intervarsity Press, 2020), 88.

because we *are* conformed to the pattern of the world and *not* naturally aligned in our hearts and minds with God. We cling to deeply held views and opinions about everything under the sun — politics, social norms, sexuality, education, and all sorts of other things. Over time, we establish our identity in these things rather than in Christ himself, and we arm ourselves with the words of worldly philosophy rather than the Word of God. We harden our minds and our hearts within our camps and ideological schools of thought. As we retreat into the comfort of our camps, it is easy to identify someone else or another group as the enemy.

Sometimes, our conflict is not ideological but interpersonal. When we experience, or at least perceive, situations of interpersonal hurt, we can hold grudges or lash out. This quote rings true for many: "Hurt people hurt people." Intentionally or unintentionally, we can cause deep, lasting hurt in each other. In the song "You Can't Always Get What You Want," the Rolling Stones describe a woman that was "practiced in the art of deception." Over time, we can also become practiced in the arts of argument, anger, conflict, standing our ground, and/or passive aggressiveness. In these ways and others, conflict has become commonplace for many of us. We separate ourselves from others through both process and content. That is, we argue about the topics that divide us — the content — and we employ tactics and methods that deepen our separation — the process.

As you read the scripture passages for this chapter, you will see that the Bible takes the topic of peacemaking very seriously. God makes allowance for reconciliation in both content and process. A good place to start our discussion on how to approach conflict is Proverbs 15:1, "A soft answer turns away wrath, but a harsh word stirs up anger." Contrary to these words of wisdom, we often approach conflict with a high emotional response — anger, fear, disrespect. This Proverb offers a challenge to practice self-control over our own reactive words and actions (II Timothy 1:7). It is a call to approach conflict resolution with gentleness and a tender heart toward the other person (Titus 3:2). In fact, sometimes the best course of action may simply be to let the smaller things go, even when we believe ourselves to be right. Rather than making a mountain out of a molehill, sometimes the best approach with minor issues is simply to hold our tongue (Proverbs 10:19). This practical wisdom can be very difficult, especially for those given to arguing, quarreling, and self-defense. For others, holding one's tongue may be an unhelpful excuse to avoid a difficult but necessary conversation. There is a need for wisdom here. We must think our way through it, using the brain God has given us to pursue wisdom, glorify God, and bring flourishing wherever we can. In some situations, we must decide to step into the conflict. Other times, we must decide to step away from it. Either way, we are called to make the decision based on godly principles.

Although it is good and right to let many things go, scripture offers a wise approach to conflict. For example, when someone sins against us or is caught in a public transgression, we are to teach and restore that person (Galatians 6:1; Colossians 3:13). This appeals broadly to the idea that, in Christian community, we are to teach one another (Romans 15:14; Colossians 3:16). Vengeance and sustained anger are never the goal (Leviticus 19:18; Romans 12:17-21). We are not to let our anger fester or grow (Matthew 5:24, Ephesians 4:26). We are either to let the issue go or deal with it following God's model laid out for us in the Bible. Rather than escalating the conflict or seeking to shame the other person through vengeance, restoration of the relationship and growth of the offending person are always the goal. In our anger and lack of self-control, it is easy to seek revenge or justice on our own terms.

In the end, the business of vengeance belongs to the Lord, not to us, even when we have been personally offended. In the process of reconciliation, we are to teach gently, forgive abundantly, and show grace to others with Christ as our example. Our job is to make every effort toward the restoration of community. Our anger and frustration in the moment tempt us to think we are more right about things than we are. This is especially true when the discord is related to those ideological camps in which we find ourselves. In our desire to rebuke, we may need to be rebuked ourselves for the way we have approached the situation. We may be clinging to a worldly ideology more tightly than is warranted. The Apostle James offers potent insight and wisdom in James 1:19-20, "Know this, my beloved brothers: let every person be quick to hear, slow to speak, slow to anger; for the anger of man does not produce the righteousness of God." Rather than righteousness, the "anger of man" produces discord, division, and ultimately more anger.

Based upon the passages explored in this chapter, we have created a little tool for conflict resolution. Keep in mind that many books have been written on this topic. In fact, entire graduate degree programs exist in conflict resolution. This little tool is neither complete nor perfect. It is designed to be a conversation starter. Successful navigation of this guide requires prayer at each step. Ask God to change your own heart first. Ask that he would guide you through this process for his glory and not for vengeance or to prove that you are right. Ask him for self-control and a tender heart.

1. *Begin with your own heart posture.* Enter the situation with humility and respect for the other person as an image-bearer. Without inward acknowledgment of the other person's dignity in Christ, progress toward reconciliation will be difficult if not impossible.

2. *Be prepared to forgive even if they do not ask for it.* Try forgiving them even before the discussion begins. Be careful not to convince yourself of good-sounding but worldly ideas that undermine true forgiveness, such as, "I forgive you, but I will never forget what you did."

3. *Decide whether to let it go or to press in.* Are you making a mountain out of a molehill? Are you holding this person to an unreasonable standard of perfection? Make your decision and move forward with it.

4. *If you still feel that it is good and right to seek resolution, approach the other person respectfully and directly.* It is OK to

seek advice from a trusted counselor, but you should avoid gossip and conversations that will damage the other person's reputation (I Timothy 5:13). For the sake of their reputation and your own, meet privately. Do not try to resolve conflict by email or text.

5. *Once you have put the issue on the table, be a good listener.* Listen not just to what is said, but to how it is being said. Pay attention to what is not being said. Ask relevant, open-ended questions. If the person apologizes, accept it, and verbalize your forgiveness. If it is a complex matter, know that multiple meetings may be required to get to a resolution.

6. *If the person resists you, then you have another decision to make.* You can either let it go or you can escalate the situation by bringing in a trusted friend (Matthew 18:15-17). If you let it go, let them know that. Then, actually let it go. Do not say you are letting it go but then let it smolder in your heart. If you choose to press on toward resolution, introduce a third party, someone the other person trusts. Do not simply bring a bigger weapon to make your case. Choose someone that will bring a calm demeanor, maturity, and reason.

7. *If the three of you are not able to reach resolution, then, once again, you have a decision to make.* You can let it go as described above, praying that God may one day bring resolution through other means. Or, if the person is a member of your church and it is a serious matter such as a public sin, you can invite a pastor or other leader

to help bring resolution (Matthew 18:15-17). Among other options, the leaders can decide if formal church discipline is required.

This is not a perfect system and not a set of rules you must follow. It is, however, based on biblical principles. Throughout the process of conflict resolution, keep a check on your own heart as well as your words. Jesus tells us that it is not what goes into the mouth that defiles us, but what comes out (Matthew 15:18). Arriving at genuine and lasting peace in our relationships requires us to put aside our pride, anger, and desire for vengeance. We must replace these inward tendencies with humility, patience, and respect for the other person as an image-bearer of God.

## SCRIPTURE READINGS

You shall not take vengeance or bear a grudge against the sons of your own people, but you shall love your neighbor as yourself: I am the Lord. – Leviticus 19:18

When words are many, transgression is not lacking, but whoever restrains his lips is prudent. – Proverbs 10:19

A soft answer turns away wrath, but a harsh word stirs up anger. – Proverbs 15:1

# Peacemaking

Blessed are the peacemakers, for they shall be called sons of God. – Matthew 5:9

Leave your gift there before the altar and go. First be reconciled to your brother, and then come and offer your gift. – Matthew 5:24

If your brother sins against you, go and tell him his fault, between you and him alone. If he listens to you, you have gained your brother. But if he does not listen, take one or two others along with you, that every charge may be established by the evidence of two or three witnesses. If he refuses to listen to them, tell it to the church. And if he refuses to listen even to the church, let him be to you as a Gentile and a tax collector. – Matthew 18:15-17

Pay attention to yourselves! If your brother sins, rebuke him, and if he repents, forgive him. – Luke 17:3

When one of you has a grievance against another, does he dare go to law before the unrighteous instead of the saints? Or do you not know that the saints will judge the world? And if the world is to be judged by you, are you incompetent to try trivial cases? Do you not know that we are to judge angels? How much more, then, matters pertaining to this life! So if you have such cases, why do you lay them before those who have no standing in the church? I say this to your shame. Can it be that there is no one among you wise enough to settle a dispute between the brothers. – I Corinthians 6:1-5

Brothers, if anyone is caught in any transgression, you who are spiritual should restore him in a spirit of gentleness. Keep watch on yourself, lest you too be tempted. – Galatians 6:1

Be angry and do not sin; do not let the sun go down on your anger. – Ephesians 4:26

Let all bitterness and wrath and anger and clamor and slander be put away from you, along with all malice. – Ephesians 4:31

Bearing with one another and, if one has a complaint against another, forgiving each other; as the Lord has forgiven you, so you also must forgive. – Colossians 3:13

Repay no one evil for evil, but give thought to do what is honorable in the sight of all. If possible, so far as it depends on you, live peaceably with all. Beloved, never avenge yourselves, but leave it to the wrath of God, for it is written, "Vengeance is mine, I will repay, says the Lord." To the contrary, "if your enemy is hungry, feed him; if he is thirsty, give him something to drink; for by so doing you will heap burning coals on his head." Do not be overcome by evil, but overcome evil with good. – Romans 12:17-21

Know this, my beloved brothers: let every person be quick to hear, slow to speak, slow to anger; for the anger of man does not produce the righteousness of God. – James 1:19-20

## DISCUSSION QUESTIONS

1. We are called not only to love peace, but to proactively bring peace in love. Some of us avoid hard conversations while others are overly assertive. Neither of these extremes results in actual peace. Where do you fall when it comes to peacemaking?

2. What are some examples of excellent peacemaking that you have witnessed in your life? What made these examples so special? What were the outcomes?

3. In what ways do you need to grow in your practice of peacemaking? Discuss some of the ways you might pursue growth in these areas.

4. This chapter offers a seven-step process for resolving conflict and bringing peace. With your group, discuss and critique this process. How would you improve it?

5. Jesus, by living the perfect life, dying on our behalf, and defeating death in his resurrection, has brought peace between God and the people of God. Talk with your group about the idea that our peacemaking efforts reflect this greater peacemaking effort by Jesus. For example, you might talk about the idea that our peacemaking efforts are a way to worship God. What does this mean for those times when we are not making peace but are harboring anger, holding grudges, and seeking vengeance?

6. What are some ways that you, as a group, can help one another become better at peacemaking? What are some ways you can practice these skills this year so they become a habit in your life?

# 18

# UNITY AND LIKE-MINDEDNESS

We are called to be peacemakers. In Chapter 17, we explored the idea that God is calling us to resolve conflicts without harboring anger and resentment. In this chapter, we will explore the concept that peacemaking within the church involves much more than the cessation of conflict. In Christian relationships, we are not only to bring an end to conflict, but also to take the extra step of being unified and like-minded. Unity and like-mindedness are beautiful aspects of God's design for the church because they reflect his perfection, unity, and wholeness. Christ himself is the source of our unity since all Christians have him in common.

Regrettably, instead of wholeheartedly entering Christian community, we sometimes find ourselves arguing and provoking one another over things that divide the church. Using the Word of God as our foundation, we are to seek and maintain agreement with one another. We are not to stir up controversies that bring division but to be unified in our identity and mission (II Timothy 2:22-26; Titus 3:10-11). Our tendencies toward argument and division too often hinder us from fully embracing life in the local church. Too often, we hold our brothers and sisters in contempt rather than seeing ourselves profoundly aligned with them in Christ. Achieving unity and like-mindedness takes humility, forgiveness, commitment, and a willingness to become part of the local church community even when it does not perfectly align with our preferences.

To begin a study of how we, as God's people, are to be unified, we should start with God himself. Deuteronomy 6:4-9, the *Shema*, informs us that God is One. He is whole and perfect. From this starting point, we also learn that we are to love God with every bit of ourselves — with our inner person, outer person, and with all our reach in the world.[1] That is, we are also to be wholly committed to the One God. Our wholeness, personally and communally, is found in God's wholeness. The Shema then goes on to say that we should teach the truth of this One God and live according to this truth in every aspect of our lives, as we sit, stand, move, or lie down. Sitting, standing, moving, not moving — these are all the human postures. Again, this is intended to say that the love of God should be our motivation for whatever we are doing. Our life is to be marked, inwardly and outwardly, in private and in public, in its entirety by our love for the God who is

---

1. Scott Redd, *Wholehearted: A Biblical Look at the Greatest Commandment and Personal Wealth* (McLean: The Institute for Faith Work and Economics, 2016).

One. God is perfect (Psalm 18:30, 19:7). Within him, there is no division, controversy, corruption, or iniquity. He is perfectly at peace and undivided within himself. He calls us, as the body of Christ, to be one as he is One (Romans 12:4-5). He calls us to be single-minded (I Corinthians 1:10) and unified in our mission (John 17:23). The Shema gives us not only a picture of the perfect unity of God but a glimpse of what he desires for his church.

God commands unity among his people because it reflects his own wholeness. He calls us to be like-minded because it is a part of his design for flourishing. As we reflect on the perfect oneness of God, we must confess that we tend toward controversy and division rather than unity. Why? Contrary to God's design for love, we demand our own way (I Corinthians 13:5). We are willing to break the fellowship of the church by pursuing our own preferences and opinions. We cling to all sorts of ideas that make sense to us and sound good on the surface, but that ultimately serve our selfishness. We are not only willing to divide ourselves over worldly ideas, but we even come to blows over the finer points of our own beliefs!

What do we quarrel about? Everything! Despite God's clear instruction to us about unity, we fight over church buildings, chairs vs. pews, grape juice vs. wine, liturgical forms, music, preaching style, seeker sensitivity, and even the paint color. If you are familiar with the history of Israel, you will recall that God commanded the people to have a year of Jubilee every 50 years (Leviticus

25).² In the Jubilee year, the land was to lay fallow. Captives were to be set free. People were to return to their homelands and resolve outstanding financial transactions. It was meant to be a time of celebration of God's goodness, a season of rest and restoration. How did God's people respond to this amazing gift from God? In hundreds of years of history in the Promised Land, it seems that a Jubilee never happened! Rather than looking forward to and planning this amazing, once-in-a-lifetime event, divisions and discord reigned. That Israel never kept the Jubilee was cited as one of the reasons God sent his people into exile (Jeremiah 25:11-12, 29:10-14). This should be a wake-up call for us as we bicker and divide ourselves over our issues today. Rather than ignoring God's clear command for unity and like-mindedness, we should embrace it and make it an emblem for all the world to see.

There are countless ways that disunity and discord happen in the church. Consider three of them: 1) our argumentative spirit, 2) division over doctrinal issues, and 3) bringing the world's ideologies into the church. Many of us are given to bickering and arguments, at least some of the time. We not only desire to win arguments but want others to embrace us in our self-perceived rightness. For some, the topic of the argument does not even matter. They just enjoy verbal sparring, gaining the upper hand, or defeating an opponent. For others, winning the

---

2. Not surprising, there has even been division among God's people on whether the Jubilee is to be every 49 or 50 years!

argument is conceptual and inward, and they may use passive-aggressive behaviors to accomplish this. In either case, scripture guides us softly but directly: accept one another (Romans 15:7), be at peace with one another (Romans 12:16), and submit to one another in love (Ephesians 5:21). If we are trying to gain status or control through discord, or if we simply have an argumentative spirit, scripture basically just says, "Stop. Be at peace."

A second way that we break the unity of the church is through doctrinal divisions. This one may seem tricky on the surface. Are we not supposed to fight for truth? As noted in a previous chapter, one denomination wisely asks its new members to commit to the study and pursuit of "purity and peace" of the church. Purity and peace go together because without peace, the church is not actually pure. And without purity, peace is an illusion. To approach doctrinal debates, it is helpful to remember one of the lines of the Nicene Creed, adopted by the church in the fourth century: "And we believe in one holy, catholic, and Apostolic Church." With these words, we affirm that we are one church, united in Christ despite geographic, cultural, and denominational lines. The phrase "Apostolic Church" signifies that we are also connected across time and generations to the very first church in the first century. As new doctrinal questions come, they must be tested and answered by scripture and understood within the context of historical orthodoxy (I Thessalonians 5:21). Otherwise, the church will be blown around by every whim and question that comes along.

A third way we divide ourselves is by clinging to worldly ideology. In becoming followers of Christ, we have become new creations; the old has gone, and the new has come (II Corinthians 5:17). In passing from death to life, we have been bought by the blood of Christ. In Christ, we are now free to think differently than the world. We are no longer bound by its value systems and popular narratives. As we initially come into the local church, we may sense that we have little in common with its members. The truth is that we have everything in common in Christ. We are free to embrace the local church community as our own, even if we personally struggle with feeling like an outsider. As part of our newness in Christ (I Corinthians 5:17), we are free to embrace our new and shared identity in him.

This does not mean, of course, that every Christian becomes an identical robot as we join the local church. By his design, there is beautiful diversity among God's people (Acts 2:9-11; Romans 12:3-8). He calls people with different abilities, from all walks of life, every tribe and tongue, into one, united, like-minded people. Joining into this new community, we are to think differently *together*. Of course, we will not do this perfectly. As we join the local church community, we will inevitably bring the world's ideas and values with us. Like doctrinal questions, we are to test the ideas of the world against the standard of God's Word. This is very difficult because we often cannot identify these patterns in ourselves. We cling tightly to our most treasured ideas about identity, justice, marriage, mercy, politics, power, sexuality, singleness, status, wealth, and so on, even when those ideas are not aligned with scripture.

Our desire to argue, our differences over doctrine, and our tendency to remain in our ideological camps as we enter the family of God are just three ways we bring division into the church. Fortunately, God sees us in our need and calls us to something better.

How can we create unity and like-mindedness in the church? To start, we should seek to understand something of God's oneness as expressed in the Shema. Second, we must examine our own hearts. In Psalm 139:23-24, David gives words to our prayer, "Search me, O God, and know my heart! Try me and know my thoughts! And see if there be any grievous way in me and lead me in the way everlasting!" This is a prayer of submission, which is the starting place for unity and like-mindedness with God and one another. As an act of submission, we must acknowledge that our ways are not always aligned with God's ways and affirm that his are better. We must acknowledge and confess the ways that we personally break unity and like-mindedness in the church.

So, as we join a church, we must do four important things. We start by looking at ourselves, critically examining our personal tendencies to argue, stir up controversy, and bring worldly values and ideals into the church. Second, we must bring to the church all the good aspects of ourselves, the person God has made us to be, including our unique abilities, interests, and gifts. We are to bring these fully for the up-building and godly encouragement of the community. Third, rather than arguing about music styles and the programs the church offers, we must embrace the local church community and commit ourselves to active participation in it. Yes, we must choose a church wisely, but once we have made our choice, we must allow ourselves to become part of that community and even to be changed by it. We must internalize the idea that the local church is 'us' rather than 'them.' Finally, in all humility, we must commit ourselves to the pursuit of unity and like-mindedness in the church, putting away those tendencies toward arguments and controversies that divide us.

## SCRIPTURE READINGS

Hear, O Israel: The Lord our God, the Lord is one. You shall love the Lord your God with all your heart and with all your soul and with all your might. And these words that I command you today shall be on your heart. You shall teach them diligently to your children, and shall talk of them when you sit in your house, and when you walk by the way, and when you lie down, and when you rise. You shall bind them as a sign on your hand, and they shall be as frontlets between your eyes. You shall write them on the doorposts of your house and on your gates. – Deuteronomy 6:4-9

Behold, how good and pleasant it is when brothers dwell in unity! It is like the precious oil on the head, running down on the beard, on the beard of Aaron, running down on the collar of his robes! – Psalm 133:1-2

I in them and you in me, that they may become perfectly one, so that the world may know that you sent me and loved them even as you loved me. – John 17:23

# Unity and Like-mindedness

For as in one body we have many members, and the members do not all have the same function, so we, though many, are one body in Christ, and individually members one of another. – Romans 12:4-5

Live in harmony with one another. Do not be haughty, but associate with the lowly. Never be wise in your own sight. – Romans 12:16

I appeal to you, brothers, by the name of our Lord Jesus Christ, that all of you agree, and that there be no divisions among you, but that you be united in the same mind and the same judgment. – I Corinthians 1:10

Finally, brothers, rejoice. Aim for restoration, comfort one another, agree with one another, live in peace; and the God of love and peace will be with you. – II Corinthians 13:11

I therefore, a prisoner for the Lord, urge you to walk in a manner worthy of the calling to which you have been called, with all humility and gentleness, with patience, bearing with one another in love, eager to maintain the unity of the Spirit in the bond of peace. There is one body and one Spirit — just as you were called to the one hope that belongs to your call — one Lord, one faith, one baptism. – Ephesians 4:1-6

Only let your manner of life be worthy of the gospel of Christ, so that whether I come and see you or am absent, I may hear of you that you are standing firm in one spirit, with one mind striving side by side for the faith of the gospel. – Philippians 1:27

So if there is any encouragement in Christ, any comfort from love, any participation in the Spirit, any affection and sympathy, complete my joy by being of the same mind, having the same love, being in full accord and of one mind. Do nothing from selfish ambition or conceit, but in humility count others more significant than yourselves. – Philippians 2:1-3

And above all these put on love, which binds everything together in perfect harmony. – Colossians 3:14

So flee youthful passions and pursue righteousness, faith, love, and peace, along with those who call on the Lord from a pure heart. Have nothing to do with foolish, ignorant controversies; you know that they breed quarrels. And the Lord's servant must not be quarrelsome but kind to everyone, able to teach, patiently enduring evil, correcting his opponents with gentleness. God may perhaps grant them repentance leading to a knowledge of the truth, and they may come to their senses and escape from the snare of the devil, after being captured by him to do his will. – II Timothy 2:22-26

As for a person who stirs up division, after warning him once and then twice, have nothing more to do with him, knowing that such a person is warped and sinful; he is self-condemned. – Titus 3:10-11

Finally, all of you, have unity of mind, sympathy, brotherly love, a tender heart, and a humble mind. – I Peter 3:8

## DISCUSSION QUESTIONS

1. What are some examples of unity and like-mindedness you have seen in the church? What makes these examples special to you?

2. Are you personally given to an argumentative spirit? If so, do you tend to have those arguments openly, or do you tend to avoid the argument but still harbor the sentiment of that argument in your heart? Explain.

3. In what ways do you feel your church is like-minded and not like-minded? Discuss.

4. Have you earnestly committed yourself to submit to church leaders? If not, discuss your reluctance. If so, describe your experience with submission.

5. The church argues within itself not only about the things the world is arguing about but also about its own things such as doctrine and matters of faith. What are some ways the church can become a lighthouse of agreement to the watching world?

6. In recent decades, it has become commonplace to critique the church and hold it in contempt for its real and perceived violations of both biblical and worldly standards of conduct. There is a good chance you

know someone that claims to be a Christian but stands apart from the church. How can we help these friends embrace the call to unity and find their place in the Body of Christ?

7. Church hopping is common among young Christian adults. Rather than leaving altogether, they hop from one church to another in search of something that makes them more comfortable. It is necessary to change churches when a body has lost its commitment to biblical truth. More often, though, people change churches because of stylistic preferences and issues of worldly ideology. Discuss the phenomenon of church hopping and how individuals can form more lasting commitments to their local church community, despite personal preferences and worldly concerns.

# SECTION 4

# LEADERSHIP

Among other things, a Fellows program is a leadership development program. It is a season to explore God's design for leaders and followers and their relationship with one another. It is a season to reflect on our call to lead and the various ways we can learn and grow as leaders.

Scripture has a lot to say about leadership and the role we are to play in the various dimensions of each other's lives — at work, at home, and at church. We are called to be encouragers who help one another grow into a deeper relationship with God. We are called to stir one another up toward love and good deeds. We are called to be Ambassadors of Christ.

This section is meant to help you explore your own calling as a leader, whether in one-to-one relationships or larger groups. As with previous sections, use the chapters as a starting point for conversation. Enrich the conversation by drawing upon the other things you are learning in your Fellows program.

# 19

# CALLED TO LEAD

In Section 3, we explored some aspects of our call to life in community as members of the body of Christ. We learned that we are called to love and serve one another by God's design and in alignment with his character. Specifically, we are called to a life of peace, unity, and likemindedness within the body of believers, working toward the shared mission of gospel flourishing.

You may be surprised to learn that scripture also calls us to lead one another. It is easy to think that leadership is something only *leaders* do. You might imagine that many, perhaps even most of us, are simply called to follow. It is true that some forms of leadership require advancement in one's career or election by others. But we would be wrong to think that only executives, managers, pastors, or elected officials are leaders or are responsible to lead. A careful reading of God's Word reveals that while not everyone is called to public leadership or vocational ministry, every follower of Christ is called to lead others in the relationships and circumstances in which God has placed them. In his book *The Leadership Formula*, Pastor Juan Sanchez writes, "Even in contexts where there are no clear relationships of authority and submission, someone will influence others toward action. [...] Someone will arise as the leader. We were made to lead and to be led."[1]

As we have seen throughout this book, God's Word not only calls us to various areas of responsibility but also equips us for the work he calls us to. Leadership is no exception to this pattern. God calls us to serve others by leading and he gives us what we need to accomplish the job.

There are many examples of our call to lead in the Bible. In this chapter, we will be looking at one of them, a passage in the book of Hebrews. Hebrews provides a helpful commentary on the temple practices of the Old Testament. In chapters 9 and 10, the author of Hebrews explains the practice of Yom Kippur, the annual Day of Atonement. This was a temple ritual established by God, described in Leviticus 16, and practiced by the Jewish people for centuries. It involved the High Priest entering the Most Holy Place of the temple and sacrificing a bull as an atonement for the sins of the people. The writer of Hebrews explains that this ritual had to be performed repeatedly, once every year. This was not because the sacrifice worked only for a while and then wore off. It was because the sacrifice *never* worked. It reflected the truth that there is not enough bull blood on earth to atone for the sins of people. It was a graphic and violent pointer to our need

---

1. Juan Sanchez, *The Leadership Formula: Develop the Next Generation of Leaders for the Church* (Brentwood: B&H Books, 2020), 7.

for a lasting sacrifice, one that would work. Until that perfect sacrifice was made, only the High Priest could enter the Most Holy Place, and even then, he did so at his own peril. The everyday people like you and me had no chance of going in there and were, metaphorically and physically, kept outside the innermost presence of God.

At this point, maybe you are asking, "all of this is interesting, but what does it have to do with leadership?" We find the answer to that question in Hebrews 10:19-25, the passage that immediately follows the description and explanation of Yom Kippur. We learn that Jesus came, made the perfect sacrifice and, in so doing, tore the curtain of the Most Holy Place from top to bottom. Because of his perfect atonement, Jesus has opened the way for us to go in and live in the presence of God, not just into a physical place on earth. Jesus' blood is the only way we can enter the presence of God.

Considering this great gift, the writer lays out three things for us to do in response:

1. *Enter with confidence* (v. 19-22). We are called to boldness (Romans 8, Hebrews 4:16), knowing that we are not only the beneficiaries of Christ's atonement, but are called by God to join him in his ongoing work. We are now with God, and he is with us.

2. *Hold fast to the truth we confess* (v. 23). As new creations in Christ (II Corinthians 5:17), we are to take up our cross each day (Luke 9:23) as living sacrifices (Romans 12:1). The old has gone and new has come (II Corinthians

5:17). We are no longer to conform to the pattern of the world, but to transform our minds (Romans 12). Scripture is our foundation of truth. It calls us to a new way of seeing, thinking, and doing, aligned with God's design and desires.

3. *Consider how to stir up one another toward love and good deeds* (v. 24). Herein lies a very clear call to leadership that every follower of Christ shares. There are no qualifications in this verse that suggest this is only applies to pastors and elders. It is a call on everyone covered by the atonement of Christ. That means you and me.

Hebrews 10:24 is a call for every Christian to lead. It begins with the charge to *consider*. Recall Chapter 3 of this book, "Called to Think." God desires us to be aligned with him inwardly and outwardly (Deuteronomy 6:4-9). We are to love God with everything inside of us, our hearts, and minds. Our thoughts are to be aligned with scripture because it expresses God's design and desires for us. Hebrews 10:24 starts with our thinking, our inner self. Specifically, it calls us to think like leaders. What must we do as leaders so that others will be stirred up to Kingdom action? What must we do to help others understand, embrace, and live out the Four-Chapter Gospel? It is, after all, in this narrative that they can find themselves and develop their sense of purpose and calling. Leaders think about their followers, collectively and individually. They think about their strengths and limitations. They think about the ways the world has influenced their thinking and the ideologies to which they cling. Leaders think about the good and bad things that motivate their followers. Without carefully thinking about their followers, leaders are less able to inspire and equip them to carry out the work they are called to do. When the writer of Hebrews calls us to *consider* how to lead, it is a call to become students of leadership.

Good thinking is essential for successful leadership, but it is not enough. The goal of good leadership thinking is good leadership action. Lord willing, good leadership action will stir others to love and good works. We are not called to simply theorize about leadership and contemplate it. We are called to practice it by inspiring and equipping one another. The phrase "stir up" in the English Standard Version is the Greek word *paroxusmos*, which means to provoke, stimulate, or goad. A goad is a stick used to poke a beast of burden, like a donkey, to go in the direction it needs to go. We are called to inspire people with the truth of the gospel, reminding them of it and admonishing them when they fall out of godly patterns in their lives. The concept of a goad implies a sense of urgency. There is work to be done, and we are to lead one another toward that work, understanding that the Kingdom of Christ is at hand.

In our leadership efforts, we can become very focused on tasks and projects, losing sight of our Kingdom mission and vision when we are blinded by the personal satisfaction that comes from success and accomplishment. The power that accompanies leadership can be dangerous for those who idolize control and the status it offers. It is important to remember that the call to stir one another up in Hebrews 10 is never a justification for selfishness, the promotion of disunity, or the adoption of worldly ideas such as "the end justifies the means." The end, or purpose, of leadership and the means of leadership are equally important in God's design because they are perfectly balanced within his character. When we choose approaches that engender fear or diminish the dignity of others, we are not leading as God has called us to lead. Hebrews 10:24 is clear that the end, or we might say measure, of our leadership is genuine love (Romans 12:9-10) and righteous deeds that have the glory of God as their goal.

  The writer of Hebrews concludes this call to leadership by saying that we are to encourage one another. Encouragement is a key component of good leadership. But what does encouragement look like? It involves the application of wisdom to every leadership situation. As we step into each other's lives with this charge to stir one another up, we are going to make leadership mistakes. And those we are leading will have their own issues as well. At times, they may ignore or resist your leadership, no matter how well-intentioned you are. People may attempt to undermine or discredit you as a leader. And, despite your best efforts, your followers may never overcome the issues that are plaguing them. As we step into leadership, we must remember that the ultimate outcomes are rarely in the control of the leader/encourager. As leaders, we must hold control loosely, acknowledging that God is ultimately in control and that the people we seek to serve are responsible for their own attitudes and actions.

At the beginning of this chapter, we noted that not everyone is called to public or elected leadership. But Hebrews 10:24-25 is a call for everyone to lead in some way. For most of us, the call to lead will apply in everyday settings of life — at home, in the church, or at work. For some, leadership will involve managing and directing groups of people. For others, it will be in individual relationships and personal friendships. For many, leadership will be a lifetime endeavor. For others, it may come in seasons. At a minimum, the call to lead will involve family relationships. While each of these situations requires unique knowledge and skills, they are linked together by the common call to stir one another up to love and good deeds. There is a lot of work to do if we are to take Hebrews 10:24-25 seriously. As we step into this responsibility, let us remember that we are loved by God, that he invites us into his work, and that leadership is part of his good design for us.

## SCRIPTURE READINGS

Where there is no guidance, a people falls, but in an abundance of counselors there is safety. – Proverbs 11:14

It shall not be so among you. But whoever would be great among you must be your servant, and whoever would be first among you must be your slave, even as the Son of Man came not to be served but to serve, and to give his life as a ransom for many. – Matthew 20:26-28

Everyone to whom much was given, of him much will be required, and from him to whom they entrusted much, they will demand the more. – Luke 12:48b

If I then, your Lord and Teacher, have washed your feet, you also ought to wash one another's feet. For I have given you an example, that you also should do just as I have done to you. – John 13:14-15

For by the grace given to me I say to everyone among you not to think of himself more highly than he ought to think, but to think with sober judgment, each according to the measure of faith that God has assigned. – Romans 12:3

Do your best to present yourself to God as one approved, a worker who has no need to be ashamed, rightly handling the word of truth. – II Timothy 2:15

Show yourself in all respects to be a model of good works, and in your teaching show integrity, dignity, and sound speech that cannot be condemned, so that an opponent may be put to shame, having nothing evil to say about us. – Titus 2:7-8

And let us consider how to stir up one another to love and good works, not neglecting to meet together, as is the habit of some, but encouraging one another, and all the more as you see the Day drawing near. – Hebrews 10:24-25

## DISCUSSION QUESTIONS

1. We often think that some people are leaders and some are not. This chapter offers the command from Hebrews 10:24-25 that we are all called to lead one another. What is your reaction to this responsibility? For example, does it energize and excite you, or does it make you fearful?

2. Hebrews 10:24-25 lays out a sequence — first, consider how to stir one another up and then do it, stir them up. This is a call to think about how to lead others. What is your reaction to this call to think about leadership? How do you feel about being a lifelong student of leadership?

3. What are some ways that you are already an effective leader? What are some ways that you need to grow as a leader? Give some examples in your discussion.

4. When we encounter a word like leadership, we often draw upon many of the world's ideas about it. We often have deeply rooted ideas about what constitutes good and bad leadership, good and bad use of power, good and bad decision-making, and so on. What are some ways that we, as followers of Christ, can transform our thoughts about leadership rather than being conformed to the pattern of the world's thinking about it?

5. Leadership happens in many different contexts. For example, we might think of public leadership in government or business. Or we might think about

leadership among friends, in the neighborhood, or in the home. The call to spur one another on to love and good deeds transcends all these scenarios. How can a leader be consistent in practicing godly leadership regardless of the forum and scope of responsibility?

6. What are some of the major challenges facing Christians as they assume leadership responsibilities within and beyond the church context? How can we prepare for and step into these challenges in a way that honors God and promotes biblical flourishing in the world around us?

# 20

# AMBASSADORSHIP

Ambassadors do not appoint themselves; they are chosen and sent by a higher authority. To be an ambassador is to have a high calling that involves important responsibilities. In II Corinthians 5:20, Paul tells us that we are ambassadors for Christ. In our study of community, we learned many ways God gathers us together. Here we also learn that he scatters us as well. King Jesus is sending us into the world as his representatives. In this way, the people of God have a unique and special role. We are called not only to talk about Jesus and the truth of his gospel but also to outwardly demonstrate it in the way we live. As we go about this work, it is important to remember that the gospel contains both the salvation message of Christ and the larger story of God's design for humanity. We are to be evangelists as the Holy Spirit provides opportunity, and we are also called to be advocates for the *missio Dei*. In our going out, we are sure to experience great joys and a sense of purpose. Scripture also says that we will face hardship and suffering as we engage with a world that does not always want to hear the message of Christ.

What does it mean to be an ambassador? An ambassador represents their *home* nation to a *host* nation, serving as a promoter and advocate. Their citizenship is in the home nation, not the host nation. Reflecting Jesus' High Priestly Prayer in John 17, we might say an ambassador is *in* the host nation but not *of* it. The word *ambassador* comes from the Latin word *ambactus*, which means high-ranking servant or emissary. The Greek word in II Corinthians 5:20 is *presbeuó*, which is an elder statesman sent to serve and represent the king. The implication is that ambassadors are servants as well as leaders. In the modern world, international diplomacy is often about what one nation can get from another. God's system is different. Ambassadors of Christ are called to give the message of redemption and flourishing to the world. We are called to share the gospel, the greatest news there is! Ambassadors of Christ go into the world to freely share the message of salvation, reconciliation with God, and a model of flourishing for the common good. They share these things in word and deed, talking about them publicly and practicing them for others to see. Professor Carl Ellis describes a four-paned window he calls the Window of Righteousness.[1] It includes four areas (i.e., panes of a window) of active gospel life: personal piety, personal justice, social piety, and social justice. He suggests that the pursuit of all four areas represents a balanced Christian

---

1. Carl Ellis, *Biblical Righteousness is a Four-Paned Window* (The Gospel Coalition, August 22, 2018).

life, lived inwardly and outwardly. By aligning our words and way of life — that is, the gospel experienced and the gospel expressed — we serve as ambassadors that demonstrate a kind of integrity that is the foundation of trust-building.

Ambassadors remain citizens of their home nation. As Christians sent into the world, we are called to ground our identity in Christ, the King who sends us. The principles of the Christian life laid out for us in the Bible reflect the culture, values, and worldview of our home Kingdom. For example, Jesus tells us, "By this, all people will know that you are my disciples, if you have love for one another" (John 13:35). Love, as defined in the Bible and displayed by Jesus, is a value that we are called to represent to the world around us. The challenge is to go into the world without conforming to its pattern or adopting its identity (Romans 12:2). As ambassadors, we must study and understand the people of our host nation. The Apostle Paul provides an outstanding example of this. While walking through Athens, he observed a statue dedicated to an unknown god. Later when speaking to the people, he said, "I perceived that in every way you are very religious people…What therefore you perceive as unknown, this I proclaim to you" (Acts 17:22-23). Paul did not accept that there is an unknown god worthy of worship. Instead, he borrowed an Athenian belief to introduce the True God. He was essentially saying, "This god that is unknown to you is known to me. He has sent me to you." This is contextualization of the gospel. It is the work of knowing the people of our host nation so well that we know how to share the gospel in ways that make sense to them. Paul's statement, "this I proclaim to you," is offered in peace and friendship. It is wisely designed to open the door to more conversation and, ultimately, to share about Jesus himself, the only hope of salvation for anyone in any nation.

Another important consideration is that ambassadors *go*; they do not stay home. They are sent as senior officials to represent the King. Some Christian groups have chosen to separate themselves from society in monastic orders or in isolated communities. This is far from God's design for us. He is sending us into the world as his representatives. We cannot hide from the culture of the world. The idea of a safe Christian bubble in which there is no worldly influence is a fallacy. We are called to live our faith publicly, as a city on a hill or a lamp on a stand (Matthew 5:14-16). People will not hear the gospel or experience the love of Christ if we do not take it to them in a visible way.

In our going out, we are sure to meet some who resist the message we carry because they do not believe the One who sent us (John 17:14). We can expect some amount of suffering and persecution as we choose to live by God's design rather than by the culture and values of the world (I Peter 4:12-19). Despite these risks, we are called to go. The Apostle Paul reminds us that our safety does not come from isolation or physical protection from persecution. Our protection comes from God himself. "If God is for us, who can be against us?" (Romans 8:31b). God equips us with the defenses we need for the work to be done — sword, shield, breastplate, helmet (Ephesians

6:10-20). These are spiritual defenses rather than physical ones.

This leads to another principle of successful ambassadorship: we must continually grow in our ability to represent Christ by growing in our knowledge and acceptance of God's Word. This growth comes through active lives of prayer and supplication, healthy and vulnerable community, corporate worship, and a commitment to regular study of scripture. God does not wait until you have the answers to all the big questions before he sends you out. He is sending you now, but he is not sending you alone. He promises to be with you, even to the end of the age (Matthew 28:20). He goes with us, and along the way, he sanctifies us, equipping us more and more for the work at hand.

A common failing among modern ambassadors is that they become locals, more aligned with their host nation than their sending nation. Ambassadors that lose sight of their purpose by serving their interests rather than the interests of their king have become foundationally corrupt. Ambassadors that adopt the interests of their host nation rather than representing the interests of their home nation are effectively traitors. In Romans 12:2, the Apostle Paul is very clear that we are "to no longer conform to the pattern of the world but transform our minds." The world's definitions of things like love, justice, mercy, peace, good, and evil can be very different from the definitions we find in the Bible. And yet, we are often drawn to the world's way of thinking because it appeals to us, seems easier, or keeps us from facing ridicule for our faith in Christ. The good news is that God knows our weaknesses and our tendency to conform to the world. He has given us his Son, the Spirit, the Word, and the community of believers. By God's grace, we are equipped to do our work as ambassadors of Christ without losing our way.

Where do the ambassadors of Christ serve? The short answer is *everywhere*. As you read this chapter, you may be tempted to think that it is a call to go abroad as a missionary. While being a missionary is good work, most Christians are not called to it. Most of us are called to work in ordinary jobs, live in ordinary neighborhoods, and do ordinary things with ordinary friends. Most of us are called to go to the place where we already live. One day per week, we are gathered as the people of God. But six days per week, we are scattered to our workplaces and neighborhoods. Knowing that the church is simultaneously gathered and scattered is an important way to understand God's design for his people.

As you consider your role as an ambassador of Christ, what do you know about the people in your workplace and neighborhood? How can you demonstrate the love of Christ to them? You show it through your hard work, diligence, commitment, and hopefulness. When they ask, "Why are you so hopeful?" you will have a ready answer (I Peter 3:15). You can also show the love of Christ by caring about them beyond the work itself. You can ask about their family and other things they care about, offering help as needed. And, of course, as the Holy Spirit provides opportunities, share the salvation message of Jesus, and invite them to church. Ambassadors of Christ *go* while staying, being in the world but not of it, prepared to share the gospel and demonstrate the love of Christ wherever they are.

## SCRIPTURE READINGS

Oh give thanks to the Lord; call upon his name; make known his deeds among the peoples! – Psalm 105:1

And I heard the voice of the Lord saying, "Whom shall I send, and who will go for us?" Then I said, "Here I am! Send me." – Isaiah 6:8

You are the light of the world. A city set on a hill cannot be hidden. Nor do people light a lamp and put it under a basket, but on a stand, and it gives light to all in the house. In the same way, let your light shine before others, so that they may see your good works and give glory to your Father who is in heaven. – Matthew 5:14-16

Go therefore and make disciples of all nations, baptizing them in the name of the Father and of the Son and of the Holy Spirit, teaching them to observe all that I have commanded you. And behold, I am with you always, to the end of the age. – Matthew 28:19-20

And he said to them, "Go into all the world and proclaim the gospel to the whole creation." – Mark 16:15

But you will receive power when the Holy Spirit has come upon you, and you will be my witnesses in Jerusalem and in all Judea and Samaria, and to the end of the earth. – Acts 1:8

For so the Lord has commanded us, saying, "'I have made you a light for the Gentiles, that you may bring salvation to the ends of the earth.'" – Acts 13:47

For I am not ashamed of the gospel, for it is the power of God for salvation to everyone who believes, to the Jew first and also to the Greek. – Romans 1:16

So faith comes from hearing, and hearing through the word of Christ. – Romans 10:17

Therefore, we are ambassadors for Christ, God making his appeal through us. We implore you on behalf of Christ, be reconciled to God. – II Corinthians 5:20

For which I am an ambassador in chains, that I may declare it boldly, as I ought to speak. – Ephesians 6:20

But our citizenship is in heaven, and from it we await a Savior, the Lord Jesus Christ. – Philippians 3:20

Continue steadfastly in prayer, being watchful in it with thanksgiving. At the same time, pray also for us, that God may open to us a door for the word, to declare the mystery of Christ, on account of which I am in prison — that I may make it clear, which is how I ought to speak. Walk in wisdom toward outsiders, making the best use of the time. Let your speech always be gracious, seasoned with salt, so that you may know how you ought to answer each person. – Colossians 4:2-6

Do your best to present yourself to God as one approved, a worker who has no need to be ashamed, rightly handling the word of truth. – II Timothy 2:15

But you are a chosen race, a royal priesthood, a holy nation, a people for his own possession, that you may proclaim the excellencies of him who called you out of darkness into his marvelous light. – I Peter 2:9

But in your hearts honor Christ the Lord as holy, always being prepared to make a defense to anyone who asks you for a reason for the hope that is in you; yet do it with gentleness and respect. – I Peter 3:15

Religion that is pure and undefiled before God the Father is this: to visit orphans and widows in their affliction, and to keep oneself unstained from the world. – James 1:27

## DISCUSSION QUESTIONS

1. Ambassadors are sent by their home nation to the host nation to represent the interests of the home nation. Our home is Christ. We are his people sent into a world that does not know him. What is your reaction to this imagery? How does it inform your way of thinking about why you are here and what Christ is calling you to do with your life?

2. Jesus says the world will know we are his by our love. The implication is that we are not simply ambassadors of words, but ambassadors of action. Our love is on display. Putting together all you have learned this year, what do you think this means practically? What are the main ways we can demonstrate the love of Christ among ourselves?

3. A common failing of diplomatic ambassadors is that they become locals. They lose sight of their home country and become indistinguishable from the citizens of their host country. What does it look like when Christians are in the world and of the world? What are some things we can do to keep our eyes on Christ even as we are sent into the world as his ambassadors?

4. When we go out as ambassadors of Christ, we will almost certainly experience great joys but also suffering. Talk about your experiences with each of these. What have been your greatest joys as an ambassador of the gospel? In what ways have you suffered?

5. We spend most of our waking hours at work. As such, the workplace is one of the many places we are sent as ambassadors of Christ. When you consider that we are representatives of the whole gospel (i.e., four chapters), what does it look like to be an ambassador of Christ at work? What are some of the ways we become indistinguishable from the world while at work?

6. When God called Moses to represent him in Pharaoh's court, he made all sorts of excuses about why God

# Ambassadorship

should pick someone else. What excuses do you make when God calls you to be his ambassador to the people in your life – at home, at work, in your friend group, etc.?

# 21

# SACRIFICIAL LEADERSHIP

In previous chapters, we explored the idea that God is calling us to be living sacrifices — fully alive and yet giving ourselves away for his glory and for the good of those around us. This idea of self-sacrifice is not just a now-and-then thing. It extends to every part of our life — including our leadership. This design by God makes perfect sense. Our approach to leadership should be informed and framed by the great value of other people and their dignity. Considering those we lead as better than ourselves (Philippians 2:3), it makes perfect sense that we would take a posture of sacrifice in our practice of leadership. As much as this design by God is beautiful and elegant, we fall short. We often see leadership as an opportunity to gain control over others, garner attention for ourselves, or obtain the social status we desire. And the world's portrayal of leaders can also be a temptation. In this chapter, let us dig into this idea of sacrificial leadership and examine our own hearts in the process.

Given the way leaders are sometimes portrayed in novels and movies, it can seem that leadership is nothing more than a way to manipulate others to get what we want.

Many have been drawn into leadership by the power and control it offers. In organizational contexts, people in leadership often make more money than individual contributors. So, in addition to the lure of power, some are drawn by greed. Clearly, our idols are alive and well in the domain of leadership. Without the right perspective, leadership can become "all about me" rather than being about those we lead and serve, not to mention the mission itself. Scripture calls us to a sacrificial lifestyle (Romans 12:1) that involves taking up our cross daily, practicing humility, and orienting ourselves toward the well-being of others. How can we develop an approach to leadership that is not motivated by selfishness? How can we truly honor the God-given dignity of those we are called to lead? How can we glorify God as sacrificial, rather than selfish, leaders?

The best place to start this study is to look at Jesus' life on earth. He provides the perfect example of sacrificial leadership. First, he left the comforts and riches of heaven, veiled his glory, and became a human being (John 6:38; II Corinthians 8:9). As a human, he took on the form of a servant (Philippians 2:5-8). Although he could have used his power in other ways, he chose to be homeless and poor (Luke 9:58; II Corinthians 8:9). In his earthly ministry, he patiently suffered the foolishness and attempted manipulations of those around him, including his own followers. He healed others (Matthew 8:16) and, despite weariness of body and heart (John 4:5-6, 13:21), pressed on doing the Father's will. In the end, he suffered greatly, even to the point of being abandoned by everyone around him. In the end, only Jesus could go to the cross. Only

Jesus, our King and leader, could pay the price for our salvation. It may be tempting to dismiss Jesus' exemplary life on the grounds that he was sinless, while we are not. We must not forget that he was fully man, tempted in all the ways we are, yet was without sin (Hebrews 4:15). In no way did he have an easier life than we do. In his call to us to follow him, Jesus invites us to take up our crosses daily (Luke 9:23). Dietrich Bonhoeffer famously wrote, "When Christ calls a man, he bids him come and die."[1] As we consider our own call to leadership, Jesus is the perfect example of what it means to be a living sacrifice. Despite incredible hardship, he stayed on his mission. He led others patiently, gently, and lovingly. While he took time to rest, he worked to the point of being tired and weary.

We can also consider leadership in terms of love — that leadership biblically understood, is an act of love. In her reflections on what it means to be made in God's image, Jen Wilkin writes, "The costliness of agape is evident in the cross. Thus those who resolve to take up their cross resolve to love as Christ loved, in a costly manner."[2] In these ways and others, we, as Christian leaders, are called to walk in his footsteps (I Peter 2:21).

---

1. Dietrich Bonhoeffer, *The Cost of Discipleship* (New York: Touchstone, 1995), 99.

2. Jen Wilkin, *In His Image: 10 Ways God Calls Us to Reflect His Character* (Wheaton: Crossway, 2018), 41.

In Philippians 2:3-4, we are instructed to do nothing out of selfish ambition but to consider others better than ourselves. This verse applies to us as leaders as much as every other aspect of life. It should shape our attitude and motivation about leading others. It is a call to humility (Colossians 3:12). It is a reminder that those we lead are made in the image of God (Genesis 1:27) and are therefore due our full respect, love, and encouragement. It is a reminder to apply the second greatest commandment, to love others as ourselves (Matthew 22:39), and to lead as we would want to be led.

Reflecting on the risks associated with sacrificial leadership, Andy Crouch writes, "Leadership begins the moment you are more concerned about others' flourishing than about your own."[3] He is saying that selfless leadership, or what we are calling sacrificial leadership, requires a willingness to take a risk. How can we do that? What would it mean to apply Romans 12:1 to your leadership practice? First, it means that we must sacrifice our selfish ambitions and vanity (Philippians 2:3). Second, it means that we are willing to suffer discomfort, if required, for the sake of the mission. Third, it means that we will give up our time, energy, and resources so that others might flourish. We should be inspired to treat those we lead with dignity, thinking of them as better than ourselves. That is, we must be careful not to dehumanize

---

3. Andy Crouch, *Strong and Weak: Embracing a Life of Love, Risk & True Flourishing* (Downer's Grove: Intervarsity Press, 2016), 111.

others by making them means to our ends. People are not simply tools or machines that produce outputs for us to enjoy. They are image-bearers with hopes, dreams, interests, and unique abilities. They have their own roles to play in the establishment of flourishing. Part of our role as leaders is to inspire and equip them to do just that.

A major challenge to our leadership is our own fallibility. For the sake of his glory and for our flourishing, God calls us to be like him — perfect (Matthew 5:48). How can this be? God is one (Deuteronomy 6:4), whole, undivided, and unchanging. He is reliable and a constant source of encouragement. In these and other ways, he calls us to be like him (Ephesians 5:1) — whole, faithful, and reliable. Our finitude will limit our reach and our fallibility will cause us to fall short of his design and desires for us as leaders. As we consider this reality, we must allow room in our leadership for grace as we fail. We must remember that we are on mission with God, and yet are sinners saved by grace.

Rather than living honestly and with integrity, the temptation for leaders is to present a very different image of themselves to the world. Leaders often try to avoid appearing weak or uncertain, instead, giving the impression that they need no help or encouragement. Many leaders feel the need to present themselves as having everything figured out. Sacrificial leadership counters this temptation by embracing authenticity. We are called to live and walk in the truth (II John 4), and our leadership is to be marked by this approach to life. Speaking to this concept, Max De Pree, the former CEO of the furniture manufacturer Herman Miller, said that it is the leader's responsibility to define reality, or what is true, for others.[4] This will take various forms as we lead. It may involve being vulnerable. It may require admitting our mistakes and asking for help. From time to time, it will almost certainly require us to ask for forgiveness from those we lead rather than ignoring or covering up our offenses against them. In this way, we not only practicing a form of authentic sacrificial leadership but leading by example. These practices are good for life and flourishing in general as well as for our work as leaders.

A sacrificial approach to leadership requires us to confront and work through various apprehensions, fears, and anxieties we have as leaders. For example, consider the leader that is overly dependent upon affirmation from those they lead. This can paralyze the leader when confronted with decisions and questions that require them to act alone. Knowing that they will not always have affirming followers with them, sacrificial leaders take steps to confront their own limitations, fears, and anxieties. They have equipped themselves to make decisions even when there is a lack of affirmation. Addressing our apprehensions, fears, and anxieties can be some of the hardest work of leadership. It is Philippians 2:3-4 in action. Putting the interests of those we lead before our own interests requires that we deal with our own failings and fears. There are many personal shortcomings that we face in leadership situations: indecision, poor communication,

---

4. Max De Pree, *Leadership is an Art* (New York: Doubleday, 1989).

analysis paralysis, blame-shifting, unrealistic expectations, and so on. Many times, these blind spots are difficult to see in ourselves. As a result, an aspect of authentic leadership is inviting others to offer advice and mentoring, especially those who see us up-close and in action.

This chapter has said a lot about what leaders must do. As you consider what is required for sacrificial leadership, it is critical to remember that our salvation is assured in Christ. Nothing that we do will earn a place for us in heaven or more of God's love. He loves us perfectly already. If you are tempted to take from this chapter a list of things you must do to earn God's love, or another list of ways that you do not measure up, take a breath. Remember Romans 8:1, "There is now no condemnation for those who are in Christ Jesus." He has already done all that is required for you to be with him. Remember that he is inviting you to be part of his great project, the *missio Dei*. He has given you all that you need: the indwelling Holy Spirit, the Word of God, and the church filled with brothers and sisters who are co-leading with you. Yes, there is much work to do, but it is the greatest work on earth.

## SCRIPTURE READINGS

Do nothing from selfish ambition or conceit, but in humility count others more significant than yourselves. Let each of you look not only to his own interests, but also to the interests of others. – Philippians 2:3-4

I appeal to you therefore, brothers, by the mercies of God, to present your bodies as a living sacrifice, holy and acceptable to God, which is your spiritual worship. – Romans 12:1

Have this mind among yourselves, which is yours in Christ Jesus, who, though he was in the form of God, did not count equality with God a thing to be grasped, but emptied himself, by taking the form of a servant, being born in the likeness of men. And being found in human form, he humbled himself by becoming obedient to the point of death, even death on a cross. – Philippians 2:5-8

For you know the grace of our Lord Jesus Christ, that though he was rich, yet for your sake he became poor, so that you by his poverty might become rich. – II Corinthians 8:9

For we do not have a high priest who is unable to sympathize with our weaknesses, but one who in every respect has been tempted as we are, yet without sin. – Hebrews 4:15

And he said to all, "If anyone would come after me, let him deny himself and take up his cross daily and follow me." – Luke 9:23

Put on then, as God's chosen ones, holy and beloved, compassionate hearts, kindness, humility, meekness, and patience, bearing with one another and, if one has a complaint against another, forgiving each other; as the

Lord has forgiven you, so you also must forgive. – Colossians 3:12

## DISCUSSION QUESTIONS

1. What are some ways that you can practice sacrificial leadership at work, at home, in friendships, and in the public square? Be specific.

2. What are some good examples of sacrificial leadership you have witnessed? What made these examples special? What did you learn from the leaders involved?

3. We sometimes talk about the virtues of living a sacrificial life, while on the inside being very focused on selfish things. When our inward and outward lives are not aligned, it is a problem of integrity. That is, we are not whole. How can we live lives of integrity in this sense? How can we align our inner thoughts and desires with our outward expression of sacrificial living?

4. Sacrificial leadership means giving up some things so those we lead may flourish. When you consider your future life, your career, your aspirations, what are the things that you cling to most and that you would find most difficult to give up?

5. Max De Pree, the former CEO of Herman Miller Furniture, wrote that it is the responsibility of the leader to define reality for others. He was referring to the idea that leaders must help others see what is real — the real

opportunities and the real challenges they face. Sometimes leaders feel compelled to exaggerate the opportunities and minimize the challenges in an attempt to motivate others. As Christians, how can we avoid these approaches in our leadership? How can we hold ourselves accountable to what is real?

6. Insecure leaders often need a lot of reassurance and affirmation from those they lead. Such leaders will often contrive environments in which they can receive the affirmation they crave. These environments and situations may be the opposite of what is actually required for the organization and people involved to flourish. How can we, as leaders, keep a check on our insecurities and unhealthy need for affirmation and reassurance? Is there a place for healthy confidence among leaders that are followers of Christ?

# 22

# INSPIRING OTHERS

What do you desire from a leader? There is probably a long list of things that you desire and even expect — integrity, kindness, clarity, etc. What about *inspiration*? At work, in the church, in politics, we expect leaders to inspire us. We expect them to call us toward a better life and a better way.

As we consider our own development as leaders, we can also embrace the opportunity to serve others by inspiring them toward God-honoring lives of love and good deeds (Hebrews 10:24). Inspiration is both a here-and-now concept as well as a forward-looking concept. In the here-and-now, leaders can help others understand that their every thought, word, and deed is important to God (Colossians 3:17). In the here-and-now, we worship God by doing all things unto him as acts of worship (Colossians 3:23). Looking to the future, leaders not only help others have perspective but also encourage them with hope that what we do today has eternal significance. Our goal is not to impress others with our brilliance, fortitude, or achievements, but to lead them to Jesus, who is the true inspiration and source of hope.

In the Bible, we are called to encourage and build one another up in the faith (I Thessalonians 5:11). What does this calling to inspire others mean for us? It means that we are called to lead nonbelievers to Jesus and to motivate and enable believers to pursue the callings God has placed on them. It means that we are called to help them along the way by carrying their burdens (Galatians 6:2). And it means that we are to encourage them toward a life aligned with God's design and desires. If we are to think about excellent and praiseworthy things (Philippians 4:8), it follows that we are also called to inspire others toward these thoughts as well.

Inspirational leadership is rooted in the Four-Chapter Gospel that we have been studying. As a starting point, leaders can help others understand the Cultural Mandate of Genesis 1:27-28. That is, we can help them understand that our efforts in this life are meant to bring flourishing, to be part of a community effort to work for the common good, and to cultivate a God-honoring society. We are to help others understand that the Fall has had far-reaching impacts, bringing toil, a sense of futility, and corruption to the things we do. We can also be a source of comfort and encouragement when those around us face the harsh realities of a broken world. Leaders have the great privilege of helping others understand that the Fall is not the end of the story. Christ has come, and Redemption is ours in him. This Good News is truly inspirational! Looking toward eternity, leaders can help others see that our labors are not in vain because we are co-laboring with Christ toward Kingdom advancement.

The Four-Chapter Gospel provides a helpful framework for considering the inspirational role of leadership.

As you read about the call to inspire others, you may be asking yourself, "What if I am not inspired myself? How can I authentically inspire others when I have my own doubts and fears?" Simply put, leadership requires us to face our doubts, fears, and indecisions without wallowing in them. The hope of the gospel is a real and present hope that transforms the mind (Romans 12:2).

The hope of the gospel saw the Apostle Paul through multiple unjust incarcerations, beatings, and other mistreatment (II Corinthians 11:23). He wrote four New Testament letters while incarcerated: Ephesians, Philippians, Colossians, and Philemon. The letter to the Philippians calls us to be joyful nearly twenty times! Philippians 4:4 famously says, "Rejoice in the Lord always; again I will say, rejoice." In living this way, Paul was neither super-human nor inauthentic. He was an ordinary person, just like you, carried along by the Holy Spirit. As leaders reading the words given to Paul by God, how can we find and share this same inspiration? In verses 11-13, he gives us the answer, "I have learned in whatever situation I am to be content. I know how to be brought low, and I know how to abound. In any and every circumstance, I have learned the secret of facing plenty and hunger, abundance, and need. I can do all things through him who strengthens me." Whether in our leading or our following, contentment can be found in Christ. Finding contentment is not an empty "prosperity gospel" promise. It is a real promise that we can embrace, even in our doubts and fears. When Paul was brought low, whether in hunger or need, he sought his strength, contentment, joy, and peace in Christ alone. Even in those times, he was able to lead others. Guided by the Holy Spirit, he penned the words we now hold dear as scripture (II Peter 3:16).

Jesus himself provides the ultimate example of leadership. Hanging on the cross, he gave words of encouragement to the thief beside him (Luke 23:43), words of comfort to his mother (John 19:26-27) and offered an intercessory prayer of forgiveness (Luke 23:34). As leaders in our homes, churches, and workplaces, we are called to inspire others, even in our weakness, by finding our strength, contentment, joy, and peace in Christ alone. He is an infinite well of inspiration that we can share with everyone we are called to lead.

The practice of inspirational leadership has two parts — an inward part and an outward part. The inward part involves our thoughts, attitudes, and values. In Philippians 4:8, Paul charges us to think about what is honorable, just, pure, lovely, etc. In other words, he is telling us to change our inner thought-life. He is acknowledging that outward change follows inward change. Rather than clinging to the thoughts that produce fear, doubt, and rebellion, we are to do some inner housekeeping. We are to replace the old thoughts with the new and beautiful truths of the gospel. As we are transformed in the power of the Spirit, we will be able to make the outward changes as well.

As we have seen with other aspects of leadership, inspiring others requires relationships and the interpersonal knowledge that flows from them. Each person you lead is unique, with unique experiences, preferences, abilities, and training. Inspiring leaders need some knowledge of these things. This knowledge will only come by knowing the people you lead at a level below the tasks at hand. Building on this concept, leadership scholars make a distinction between *transactional* leadership and *transformational* leadership.[1] Transactional leadership sees the follower in mechanistic and dehumanizing terms — simply as someone to complete tasks. Transformational leadership includes the completion of tasks but also makes room for the humanity and dignity of the follower — their hopes, dreams, and aspirations. An inspirational leader will make efforts to reach everyone at this deeper level. For example, you might lead by helping others to see the beauty and value of their work even when those efforts mainly involve ordinary, routine tasks. You might help them to see the ways that their efforts contribute to the larger picture. You might encourage them to see the unique ways that they contribute to the culture and camaraderie of the team.

    Do these ideas challenge you? As you near the end of your Fellows program, we want you to embrace this challenge. In Section 2 of this book, you were encouraged to see yourself as a servant. Now, in Section 4, you are being encouraged to see yourself as a leader. In fact, you are encouraged to see yourself as a servant leader that

---

1. J.M. Burns, *Leadership* (New York: Harper & Row, 1978).

makes sacrifices for the good of others. In this chapter, you may find yourself resisting the call to inspire others because doing so will require you to sort out some of your own fears, doubts, and cynicism. Be encouraged! Jesus already knows about these things. He stands waiting to meet you as you confront them. As he was with Paul, Jesus is your strength and joy. In him, you can lead in a way that encourages and inspires others, even as you face your own issues. Jesus is calling all his people to lead each other in some way (Hebrews 10:24) — we are all in this together, the community he created us to be, working for his glory and to increase flourishing in the world.

## SCRIPTURE READINGS

Bear one another's burdens, and so fulfill the law of Christ. – Galatians 6:2

Rejoice in the Lord always; again I will say, rejoice. – Philippians 4:4

Finally, brothers, whatever is true, whatever is honorable, whatever is just, whatever is pure, whatever is lovely, whatever is commendable, if there is any excellence, if there is anything worthy of praise, think about these things. – Philippians 4:8

Not that I am speaking of being in need, for I have learned in whatever situation I am to be content. I know how to be brought low, and I know how to abound. In any and every circumstance, I have learned the secret of facing plenty and hunger, abundance and need. I can do all things through him who strengthens me. – Philippians 4:11-13

And whatever you do, in word or deed, do everything in the name of the Lord Jesus, giving thanks to God the Father through him. – Colossians 3:17

Whatever you do, work heartily, as for the Lord and not for men, knowing that from the Lord you will receive the inheritance as your reward. You are serving the Lord Christ. – Colossians 3:23-24

Therefore encourage one another and build one another up, just as you are doing. – I Thessalonians 5:11

And let us consider how to stir up one another to love and good works, not neglecting to meet together, as is the habit of some, but encouraging one another, and all the more as you see the Day drawing near. – Hebrews 10:24-25

## DISCUSSION QUESTIONS

1. What leadership traits and practices are most inspirational to you? Why do you find these things inspirational? Do you practice these things yourself?

2. Do you agree with the premise of this chapter —that leaders are expected to inspire those they lead? Explain your thoughts on this.

3. Leaders sometimes find it difficult to inspire others when they, themselves, are not inspired about the task at hand. Burnout and lack of vision are often cited as reasons leaders lack inspiration. But, for Christians, perhaps we have lost sight of the nearness of Christ in all we do. His presence is our inspiration, whether the task is big and exciting or small and ordinary. Share with the group a time that you were uninspired about a task. Would a better sense of Christ's presence in the task have changed your view? How can we as leaders confront and counteract this lack of vision in ourselves?

4. Inspiration requires being able to envision the future. Clearing a weedy area of your yard is not usually a very fun project. The inspiration to get it done is not the fun of the work, but the outcome: a beautiful new garden. Sometimes a leader's job is to help people see that the work will result in a good outcome (vision-casting). And yet, we live in a tech-laden, short-attention-span, entertainment culture. How can a leader help people see beyond the discomfort of short-term tasks to be motivated by the longer-term outcomes?

5. On many teams, there is often someone like Eeyore from the Winnie-the-Pooh stories. No matter what the leader does, this individual cannot see the good in it. Their negativity is often a wet blanket on a team. What can a leader do about the Eeyore that strongly resists any attempts at genuine inspiration?

6. Consider inspirational leadership in the church setting. There is an saying that 20 percent of people do 80 percent of the work in a local church (i.e., the famous "80-20 Rule"). What are some ways that you, as a lay leader in the church, could impact and improve upon the 80-20 rule? What are some ways you could inspire others and influence them to be more involved in the work of your local church? What excites you about this? What intimidates you about it?

# 23

# LEADING IN THE CHURCH

We are called to lead and serve one another in every dimension of life — at home, at work, in the neighborhood, and in society. We are also called to lead one another in the church. As with other leadership roles, leadership in the church can be formal or informal. Informal leadership might involve walking with someone through difficult times or spiritual doubts. It might mean praying, comforting, providing meals, and so on. To a very large extent, the church thrives on these informal, self-initiated relationships. Formal leadership in the church typically involves a process of selection or election, depending on your denomination and its system of polity. The selection process follows the biblical directive to "choose among yourselves" (Deuteronomy 1:13; Acts 6:3, 15:22) those who would serve as leaders. This chapter will primarily address formal leadership roles in the church.

If you are new to the church, you may wonder how one becomes a leader. If you grew up in the church, you may not have thought of yourself as a leader and may also wonder how someone becomes a leader. Very broadly, there are four types of leadership roles in the modern

Protestant church: ordained vocational leadership, ordained lay leadership, non-ordained lay ministry leadership, and non-ordained church staff. There is a lot of variation among denominations, but generally, these are the types of leadership roles you will find in a modern church.

1. *Ordained vocational leaders* are most often paid church staff who have the responsibility to teach and lead the congregation. Depending on the denomination, these might be senior pastors, assistant pastors, rectors, or assistant rectors. Ordained vocational leaders typically have specialized training and graduate degrees in theology, biblical languages, or related disciplines.

2. *Ordained lay leaders* are usually ruling elders and deacons. They might be known as members of the session, vestry, or consistory, depending on the denomination. Ordained lay leaders are responsible for the spiritual and practical oversight of the local church as well as the oversight of outreach, missions, and service ministries. These roles do not typically require formal education in theology and are generally unpaid.

3. *Non-ordained ministry leaders* can vary significantly from church to church and even within a church. Some examples of non-

ordained ministry leaders: small group leaders, youth ministry servants, prayer team leaders, wedding and funeral care leaders, missions team leaders, etc. Non-ordained ministry leaders are generally not paid for their service and most often do not have formal education in theology.

4. *Non-ordained church staff* roles vary from church to church. Common non-ordained staff you might see in a church are leaders of youth and children's ministries, global and local missions, congregational and family care, counseling, "age and stage" communities (e.g., young adults, seniors), worship, communications, and finance. Church staff often have specialized training and are paid for their work.

Why list all these roles here? As a Fellow nearing the end of your program year, you should consider that God may be calling you to one or more of these roles. You may find a new small group in your church community that needs a leader. You may be interested in leading a vision trip to encourage and support one of your church's missionaries. You may feel called to work with children or youth. Paul calls each of us to use our unique gifts as members of the body of Christ (Romans 12:6-8). As you complete your Fellows year, prayerfully consider where God would have you serve and lead.

When considering formal leadership roles in the church, potential leaders must assess their own motivations. The ideal motivation for serving as a church leader is the desire to glorify God, to advance his Kingdom, and to bring more flourishing into the world. No leader will perfectly pursue or embody these motivations. In most churches, leaders are asked to pursue the welfare of the local church and agree with the main tenets of its doctrine. In addition, all leaders in the church, regardless of their primary role, share some responsibility to make the church an inviting and welcoming place for visitors, especially those that are exploring Christianity for the first time.

Thinking back to Chapter 16, you may recall that your responsibility as a member of a church is to fully join in, embrace the local church, and bring your abilities to the work of that congregation. As a leader in the local church, you will need to go beyond joining in. You will need to help create an environment where others can join in. You will have the additional requirement to be a public advocate for biblical truth (Ephesians 4:25) and genuine love (Romans 12:9).

To understand Jesus' views on how we are to lead and serve, Matthew 10 presents a good model for us. It contains his instructions to the disciples as he sent them out to do his work. The first observation is that he said to them, "Go! Interact with people." He was not telling them to huddle behind closed doors. Second, he instructed them to proclaim that the Kingdom of Heaven is at hand. In other words, they were to share the good news of the gospel — the parts people wanted to hear and the parts they did not want to hear. Jesus told them to be as wise as serpents and as innocent as doves because he was sending them out as sheep among wolves. Not everyone they met was a wolf seeking to do them harm, but some were. As a leader in the church, you must also be wise like a serpent and innocent like a dove for the same reasons.

Leadership in the church requires self-motivation and personal drive. Borrowing from a concept developed in the nineteenth century by William Forster Lloyd, ecologist Garrett Hardin coined the phrase "tragedy of the commons" to describe a communal environment in which no one takes personal responsibility for the care and upkeep of a shared resource.[1] For example, imagine an apartment with four roommates. Who is responsible to clean the kitchen? Who is responsible to remove the trash? Without a conversation that clarifies who is responsible for these things, it is likely that they either will not get done or the tasks will fall to the one conscientious person who will do them. Roommates can resolve these problems with a conversation and an agreement with one another. But what about new things that arise that the roommates did not anticipate, things that were not included in the conversation? Or what about the roommate who does not care all that much about violating the agreement? In a sense, the church is a Commons, a set of resources and initiatives that are held in common for the advancement of

---

1. Garrett Hardin, "The tragedy of the commons." *Science* 162(3859), 1968.

the Kingdom. As such, a church can be subject to the tragedy of the commons. Being a leader in the church means assuming a sense of responsibility for it, its people, and its work. It means not just thinking about that responsibility on a conceptual level but being willing to take actual responsibility for things and to apply your gifts to the ministry needs. Sometimes the need is simply to show up and do the things that are unseen, ordinary, or outside of our comfort zones.

Your Fellows year is nearly over. You have had a long season of training and development. Now is the time to go and find your place as both a member and leader in your church. Take the initiative by asking the pastoral staff or other leaders where the needs are and then step in to lead and serve there. Take the initiative to become a student of that area, whether in youth ministry, missions, ESOL, or care ministries. Start by learning and serving under the leadership of others. Then, as your knowledge and experience grow, start to take on more leadership responsibility. Be comforted by the words of Romans 8. You are an heir of God the Father. If he is for you, nothing can be against you. So, go and figure out what your place of servant leadership is and then get after it.

## BIBLE READINGS

Choose for your tribes wise, understanding, and experienced men, and I will appoint them as your heads.
– Deuteronomy 1:13

These twelve Jesus sent out, instructing them, "Go nowhere among the Gentiles and enter no town of the Samaritans, but go rather to the lost sheep of the house of Israel. And proclaim as you go, saying, 'The kingdom of heaven is at hand.'" – Matthew 10:5-7

Therefore, brothers, pick out from among you seven men of good repute, full of the Spirit and of wisdom, whom we will appoint to this duty. – Acts 6:3

Then it seemed good to the apostles and the elders, with the whole church, to choose men from among them and send them to Antioch with Paul and Barnabas. They sent Judas called Barsabbas, and Silas, leading men among the brothers. – Acts 15:22

For all who are led by the Spirit of God are sons of God. For you did not receive the spirit of slavery to fall back into fear, but you have received the Spirit of adoption as sons, by whom we cry, "Abba! Father!" – Romans 8:14-15

Let love be genuine. Abhor what is evil; hold fast to what is good. – Romans 12:9

Therefore, having put away falsehood, let each one of you speak the truth with his neighbor, for we are members one of another. – Ephesians 4:25

## DISCUSSION QUESTIONS

1. This chapter introduces some categories of leadership roles in the church: ordained vocational leadership, ordained lay leadership, non-ordained lay ministry leaders, non-ordained church staff. These can vary by denomination and church. What are some roles in your home church?

2. As noted in a previous chapter, it is often said that "20 percent of the people do 80 percent of the work" in the church. Do you believe this is true? Why or why not? If it is true, what steps can you take for this to be different as you step into adulthood in the church?

3. How has your Fellows year prepared you for servant leadership in the church? How has your service in the local church this year taught and formed you? In what ways do you plan to serve in your local church after your Fellows year?

4. As a leader in the church, you will be held to the often-competing standards of others. Sometimes, people will expect you to be above reproach (even when they are not). Other times, people will expect you to be "real" and "authentic," which can be a euphemism for being transparent about your personal failings. What are some ways you can navigate the push and pull of competing expectations as a leader in the church?

5. Leadership in the church often requires stepping into deeply personal matters with others as they wrestle with

painful situations in their lives. These might range from doubts about God's love to the lingering effects of trauma and abuse. On one hand, their experiences may be so unfamiliar that the leaders involved can have a deep sense of inadequacy in walking with them. On the other hand, the experiences may hit very close to home with leaders who have had similar experiences. In both cases, leaders need to be prepared to deal with whatever comes their way. What are some strategies church leaders can employ to walk with others through difficult things while also taking care of themselves? What are some areas that for you will require special preparation and care?

6. You have had the chance to think about the stresses, challenges, and joys of leadership in the church. Hopefully during this year, you have been part of several leadership opportunities. How has this season impacted your sense of calling as a leader in the church? How has it impacted your views of church leaders you have observed this year or earlier in your life?

7. God loves us so much that he gave us his Son. In ascending to heaven, Jesus sent the Holy Spirit to indwell us, comfort us, and teach us. In the church, he also gives us leaders and calls us to lead others. Have you considered that those who lead you are a gift from God and that you, as a leader, are a gift to others? Discuss.

# 24

# FINAL REFLECTIONS

Here we are at the end of your Fellows program. Well done! Even though you have reached the end of your Fellows year, you have not reached the end of learning about God's call on your life. In many ways, the final days of the Fellows year mark a beginning rather than an end. We often say, "Once a fellow, always a fellow." This simply means that our hope for you is a lifetime of growing and learning. The Fellows year is meant to be an introduction to themes that you will pursue the rest of your life. To that end, this brief closing chapter offers three tips for continuing your study.

*Tip One – Remember that Jesus is the center of it all.* A key point, in fact *the* key point of your Fellows year is that Jesus is the center of it all. If he is who he claims to be in John 1, Colossians 1, and Hebrews 1, then there is no aspect of this life that is not under his Lordship. There is no aspect of life that does not involve him. There is no aspect of life that is not an opportunity to worship him. He made you in his image, with purpose and responsibility. So go into all you do remembering that he is with you. Be bold, knowing that he has paved the way for you and that eternal life in him has already begun. He is calling you to join in all that he is doing to create, sustain, and re-create.

*Tip Two – Be encouraged in this life.* Sometimes we think that Christians are supposed to be somber and woeful. As we bump into the hardships of life in a broken world, we can easily lose sight of the overwhelming joy that is ours in Christ. Remember that Jesus prayed that we would have joy (John 17). Do you think this prayer was answered by the Father? The intent of that prayer was not that we would be dancing, giddy people all the time. Even Jesus wept when it was time to mourn. But he did not live a life of mourning. He enjoyed his friends and eagerly sought out the work he was called to do. Follow in his footsteps in this regard. Enjoy your life and let others see that you have great hope. Through your work and attitude, let them see that you have a sense of God-given purpose and motivation in your life. Inspire them to ask the question, "How is it that you can have so much hope?" Let yourself be happy because Jesus loves you so much.

*Tip Three - Step in and step out.* We learned in this study that we are called to be gathered at times and scattered at other times. Whether gathered or scattered, we are called to be in Christ, living for his glory and for the flourishing of those around us. We are called to be gathered in the local church, part of the family, committed, and serving despite its shortcomings. We are called to actively step into the life of the church. We are not to be tourists or consumers in the church. Rather than seeing the church as something that primarily gives to us, we are to see it as a place where we give ourselves, working together with fellow believers in our shared mission. In addition to our time gathered, we are also called to scatter. We are called to go into our neighborhoods, workplaces, schools, and the public square. God has called us to go as his ambassadors. We are called to go, knowing that we will face opposition at times. Despite the potential for opposition, we are called to show God's love, serving into the needs around us and even being willing to forgo our own comfort and preferences. As we go, we are called to remain faithful to Christ, clinging to the truth of scripture rather than adhering to the values and ideologies of the world around us. We are called to actively step into life in the church and actively step out into life in the world, all while keeping Jesus front and center.

Congratulations on a year well done! In all your callings — to love, think, work, serve, lead — take the lessons of this year with you. You are a student of all these things in a school of lifelong learning. Take note of the fact that the Fellows learning model involves head, heart, and hands. As you continue to grow, keep these in balance by feeding your mind and heart and by engaging your hands in the work of the Kingdom. May God bless you richly as you go.

# ACKNOWLEDGEMENTS

No one writes alone. There are many people to thank for making this book possible. I will start by thanking the staff and board of the Second Presbyterian Church Foundation for their generous support of TFI's curriculum initiative. Without your support, this book and the other TFI curriculum materials simply would not be possible. I especially want to thank Vicki Simmons, Executive Director of the Second Presbyterian Church Foundation. Vicki, your encouragement, support, and friendship have been an incredible blessing over the years. Thank you!

I am grateful to Luke Bobo, James Forsyth, and Bill Fullilove for reviewing and improving the manuscript. Even though you had your own deadlines and challenges, all of you were willing to be part of this project. Your insights have made it much better. I am also thankful for Anna Arnold and Celeste Ava, who served as copyeditor and proofreader, respectively. Thank you, Anna and Celeste, for your careful work and thoughtful insights.

Alaina Conley read the early drafts. Her insight as a fellow and colleague at TFI has been very helpful. I would like to thank the Capital Fellows who talked through so much of this material over the years. I am grateful to all of you! Shirley Kyle, my patient wife, was an integral part of developing and sharing this material over the last decade. She also reviewed the manuscript and offered many insights along the way.

Finally, I would like to thank the board of TFI, chaired by Dr. Ken Friday. The board is a wonderful team that has faithfully supported this important ministry with prayer and personal sacrifice. Thanks to all of you!

# ABOUT TFI

The Fellows Initiative (TFI) is a growing network of Christian discipleship and leadership development programs for recent college graduates. Our mission is to inspire and equip the emerging generation of leaders for the marketplace, church, and society.

TFI Fellows programs share a commitment to Jesus Christ, his Word, and his church. We encourage fellows toward lives of servant leadership marked by the seamless integration of faith, work, service, and community. We are committed to promoting biblical flourishing in the world.

With more than thirty years of experience developing, launching, and leading Fellows programs, TFI provides training, best practices, coaching, and support to churches that want to launch and lead Fellows programs in their local contexts. By God's grace, TFI has grown to be a coast-to-coast network of programs that not only equips young leaders but transforms churches.

Learn more at thefellowsinitiative.org.

Made in the USA
Columbia, SC
12 April 2024